JOSEPH WITTLIN

Pub 4.76

TWAYNE'S WORLD AUTHORS SERIES

A Survey of the World's Literature

Sylvia E. Bowman, Indiana University

GENERAL EDITOR

POLAND

Adam Gillon, State University of New York College
at New Paltz
Ludwik Krzyzanowski, New York University

EDITORS

Joseph Wittlin

(TWAS 224)

TWAYNE'S WORLD AUTHORS SERIES (TWAS)

The purpose of TWAS is to survey the major writers—novelists, dramatists, historians, poets, philosophers, and critics—of the nations of the world. Among the national literatures covered are those of Australia, Canada, China, Eastern Europe, France, Germany, Greece, India, Italy, Japan, Latin America, the Netherlands, New Zealand, Poland, Russia, Scandinavia, Spain, and the African nations, as well as Hebrew, Yiddish, and Latin Classical literatures. This survey is complemented by Twayne's United States Authors Series and English Authors Series.

The intent of each volume in these series is to present a critical-analytical study of the works of the writer; to include biographical and historical material that may be necessary for understanding, appreciation, and critical appraisal of the writer; and to present all material in clear, concise English—but not to vitiate the scholarly content of the work by doing so.

Joseph Wittlin

By ZOYA YURIEFF
New York University

Twayne Publishers, Inc. :: New York

To the memory of
Wladyslaw Michniewicz who
perished in World War II

Contents

Preface

The aim of this book is not to introduce, but rather to reintroduce to a wider American audience a distinguished Polish writer, Joseph Wittlin, author of an important war novel *The Salt of the Earth*,* now published for the third time in English. He also is a fine poet, essayist, and an outstanding translator of the *Odyssey* from Homer's Greek into Polish hexameters. He has been known in this country since 1941, when his novel appeared in New York, and especially since 1943, when he became the first Polish writer to receive the award of the American Academy of Arts and Letters. In the same year he was also honored by the National Institute of Arts and Letters. *The Salt of the Earth (Sól ziemi)*, a book which can be read on many levels, became an international bestseller in the latter half of the 1930's and was translated into 13 languages long before it became fashionable to translate new and significant books into other languages almost simultaneously with their appearance in the original. "Anyone who does not know Wittlin does not know Polish literature," wrote a critic in an important German newspaper, *Die Zeit*, on the appearance of a new German edition of the novel.

A laureate of the Polish Academy and a candidate for the Nobel Prize in 1939, he settled in 1941 in Riverdale, N. Y. and has been living there ever since. His books, including the third version of his *Odyssey* which was eagerly awaited by Polish critics and readers, are barred from Poland. This is the primary reason why no book-length critical study has been published on Wittlin, although numerous articles in several languages have been devoted to him and to his work.

---

*Giniger, Harrisburg, Pa.: Stackpole Books, 1970.

This study, which is a pioneering effort to analyze and appraise Wittlin's work, does not pretend to be exhaustive or definitive. It seeks to give the English-speaking reader only a brief insight into the life and work of an outstanding modern Polish writer in exile.

Critical material on Wittlin is scarce in this country and had to be obtained largely from Poland. Very few translations of his exquisite poetry are available in English. Some quotations, especially in Chapters I and II, had to be translated, thus limiting my possibilities for a "microanalysis" of the poetry. Fortunately there is a translation of *The Salt of the Earth* into English, reprinted in Harrisburg, Pa.

A tendency to perfect his writing with painstaking effort pervades all of Wittlin's work. Indeed, his work cannot possibly be divided along chronological lines. Three different versions of the *Odyssey* came out in 1924, 1931, and 1957, respectively. Moreover, the three editions of the *Hymns* differ from each other in the number and individual make-up of their constituent poems. Recently Wittlin, who is now preparing the second volume of his *Collected Works*, revised his old poetry producing new versions of it. Early books, *War, Peace and a Poet's Soul* (Wojna, pokój i dusza poety, (1925), and *Stages* (Etapy), (1932), are included in part in the book of essays *Orpheus in the Inferno of the Twentieth Century* (Orfeusz w piekle XX wieku), (Paris, 1963).

Thus separate chapters in this book are devoted to Wittlin's poetry, to his translation of the *Odyssey* (all three versions), his prose and his essays. Generally speaking, my approach has been of an analytical rather than a biographical nature, although certain biographical data were included when pertinent to his work. I have attempted to show the evolution of Wittlin as poet, translator and essayist.

Grateful acknowledgment is due to Professors Wiktor Weintraub (Harvard University), and Zbigniew Folejewski (University of British Columbia), both of whom made valuable suggestions. I am also indebted to the late Professor Robert Magidoff, formerly Head of the Department of Slavic Languages and Literatures, New York University, and to his successor, Professor Andrej Kodjak, for providing me with copy-editing help. I thank Dr. Alfred Berlstein, formerly of the Slavonic Division of The New York Public Library, for his aid in procuring some valuable material from Poland. I wish to thank especially James

Preface

E. A. Woodbury, for a painstaking revision of my English and
Adam Gillon and Dorothy Meller for their translations of some
of Wittlin's poems. Others who have rendered help in the editing
of the book are: William S. Hathaway, David Frohlich, my sister
Valerie Filipp and my husband, George Yurieff, who prepared
the Bibliography and Index. I thank Professor Adam Gillon and
Professor Ludwik Krzyzanowski for reading the manuscript and
for their helpful suggestions, and Professor Leon Tadeusz
Blaszczyk for having read and commented on Chapter 3.

ZOYA YURIEFF

New York University
June, 1971

Chronology

1896   Józef (Joseph) Wittlin is born in Dmytrów (district Radziechów) in northeastern Galicia. Father, Karol Wittlin, mother, Elisabeth, née Rosenfeld.

1906- Attended a classical Gymnasium in Lwów.
1914

1912   First poem published in a youth magazine *Wici* (Beacon) in Lwów.

1914   Volunteered for the Eastern Polish Legion.

1915   Diploma from a Gymnasium in Vienna.

1915- Studied philosophy at the University of Vienna.
1916

1916- Served in the Austro-Hungarian Army as a private and
1918   then as an officer-cadet.

1918   Returned to Lwów. Studied at the University of Lwów.

1919- Taught Polish Language and Literature at Gymnasium in
1921   Lwów.

1919- Affiliated with the Group of Polish Expressionists in Poz-
1920   nan, *Zdrój* (The Spring).

1920   First collection of poems, *Hymns*, published in Poznan.

1921- Moved to Lódz and became a literary director at the Mu-
1924   nicipal Theater there. Lectured at the School of Drama in Lódz of which he was cofounder.

1922   A new version, a paraphrase of *Gilgamesh*, the Old Babylonian epos, published in Lwów.

1924   Married Halina Handelsman.

1924   A translation of Homer's *Odyssey* from Greek into Polish published in Lwów, a literary success for Wittlin.

1925   A book of essays and addresses *War, Peace and a Poet's Soul* is published in Zamosc. Work on the first part of a trilogy about World War, *The Saga of the Patient Foot-soldier.*

1925- Stayed in Italy, in Assisi. Worked on a book about Saint
1926   Francis of Assisi, fragments of which were published in
       1927, 1931 and 1932.

1927   Moved to Warsaw; writes, translates, adapts from Italian
       and German. Contributes to leading periodicals and news-
       papers.

1928   First visit to France, a country which becomes very close
       to the author's heart. Travels in Western Europe.

1931   Second version of *The Odyssey* appeared in Warsaw.

1932   Daughter, Elisabeth, is born.

1933   A book of travel sketches, *Etapy* (Stages), published in
       Warsaw.

1935   Award from the Polish PEN-Club for the second version
       of the *Odyssey.*

1935   *The Salt of the Earth,* the first part of the *Saga of the
       Patient Footsoldier,* published in Warsaw, achieves great
       literary success.

1936   *The Salt of the Earth* is awarded a double prize by the
       so-called Academy of the Independents of the leading
       literary magazine *Wiadomosci Literackie* and by its read-
       ers, as the best book of 1935.

1937   German and a Dutch translations of *The Salt of the Earth*
       are published in Amsterdam.

1937   Awarded Golden Laurel by the Polish Academy of Liter-
       ature. A Czech and two Russian translations of *The Salt
       of the Earth* are published.

1939   An English, a French and an Italian version of *The Salt
       of the Earth* are published in London, Paris and Milan.

1939   A journey to a retreat for writers in the Foyer de l'Abbaye
       de Royaumont near Paris to work on the second part of
       The Saga of the Patient Footsoldier. The outbreak of
       World War II. A Swedish version of *The Salt of the Earth*
       appears in Stockholm.

1940   Mrs. Halina Wittlin and daughter join Mr. Wittlin in
       Paris. Flight to the South of France. In June 1940 loss of
       manuscripts and materials for the continuation of *The
       Saga,* while waiting for a boat to England in St. Jean de

Luz. A Croatian translation of *The Salt of the Earth* published in Zagreb.

1940   Arrived in Portugal.

1941   Sailed for the U.S.A. in January.

1941   A second English edition of *The Salt of the Earth* published in New York.

1941-   Coeditor of the New York Polish weekly *Tygodnik Polski.*
1943

1943   *The Salt of the Earth* is awarded a prize by the American Academy of Arts and Letters and by the National Institute of Arts and Letters in New York. A Spanish translation of *The Salt of the Earth* appears in Buenos Aires.

1943-   Coeditor of *The Democratic Heritage of Poland. For*
1944   *Your Freedom and Ours.* An Anthology of Polish Democratic Thought. Two editions in London (1943 and 1944) and one in New York (1943).

1945   A Polish edition of the above Anthology published in New York.

1946   *Mój Lwów* (My Lwów), a book of memoirs, published in New York.

1948   A Polish translation of John Hersey's *Hiroshima* published in Warsaw.

1952   Work for Radio Free Europe.

1954   A new Polish edition of *The Salt of the Earth* appeared in New York.

1957   A third, completely revised version of the Polish *Odyssey* was published in London.

1963   *Orpheus in the Inferno of the Twentieth Century (Orfeusz w piekle XX wieku),* a book of essays and other prose writings in Polish was published in Paris.

1965   Awarded a prize by the Jurzykowski Foundation in New York for his entire creative output.

1969   A new edition of *The Salt of the Earth* in German is a major literary success in Germany and Austria.

1971   Chosen a Corresponding Member of the Deutsche Akademie für Dichtung und Sprache (German Academy of Poetry and Language), Darmstadt, West Germany.

CHAPTER I

Early Background and Early Poetry

Wer Religion hat,
Wird Poesie reden.*
Friedrich Schlegel.

IN the year 1969 Joseph Wittlin, the eminent Polish writer—
poet, essayist and translator—completed half a century of
creative work. Had he been able to return after World War II
to a Poland which would have welcomed him back, this would
have been a widely celebrated occasion. But in fact he was
obliged to spend the anniversary of his literary debut in exile,
in Riverdale, New York, and only his voice reached across the
ocean over Radio Free Europe, of which he is a highly valued
associate. A true democrat—a rare species in Eastern Europe
(or, for that matter, anywhere)—who is repelled by all forms of
totalitarianism and suppression of human freedom, Wittlin has
refused many tempting invitations to return to his native country
since the war. In 1948 Wittlin's translation of John Hersey's
Hiroshima was published by Wiedza Publishers in Warsaw. The
censors of the Polish People's Republic deleted Wittlin's Preface
to the book, which they replaced with a demagogical Afterword
by a Party member. This was warning enough for Mr. Wittlin.
He has preferred free speech ever since he began writing.

In 1919 he published a poem, "Lullaby," addressed to those
who had been killed in the Great War which had wrecked half
the world. This poem, published in the limited-circulation magazine *Zdrój* (The Spring), the organ of the Polish Expressionists in Poznan, was included in his first collection of poetry,
Hymns, which appeared in 1920, also published by *Zdrój,* and

---

**He who has religion*
Will speak poetry.

was promptly sold out. A second, somewhat altered edition, followed in 1925, and a third one in 1929 printed by J. Mortkowicz.[1] Recently some of the hymns were reprinted in a Polish magazine published in London, *Oficyna Poetów i Malarzy* (Poets' and Painters' Press),[2] which appeared as a tribute to the "grand seigneur of Polish letters," as the younger Polish writer Tadeusz Nowakowski referred to Wittlin in a review of the latter's masterpiece *The Salt of the Earth*, now issued for the first time in Germany (though for the second time in a German translation).[3] Nowakowski says in the review that whoever does not know Wittlin does not know Polish literature.[4] But in contrast we can point to the recently published extensive *History of Polish Literature* by Julian Krzyżanowski, in which Wittlin's name is completely omitted,[5] as are the names of many other prominent émigré poets and writers. Julian Krzyżanowski, although on the surface seeking to arrive at an objective appraisal of Polish literature throughout the world[6] has taken it upon himself to omit Józef Wittlin's name not only as a poet and translator into Polish of Homer's *Odyssey*, but also as a prose writer, whose *The Salt of the Earth* was an international best seller in the 1930's. One can find an explanation for this oversight in the Polish Biographical Dictionary, where Wittlin and his bibliography occupy several pages but where the compiler also mentions Wittlin's cooperation with magazines and newspapers which are "hostile to The Polish People's Republic."[7]

Fortunately for the foreign reader and scholar another extensive study, *The History of Polish Literature*, appeared at almost the same time as Krzyżanowski's book, in which the author, a Polish poet, critic and essayist of international repute, Czeslaw Milosz (b. 1911), comments on Wittlin's *The Salt of the Earth* and on his poetry:

The novel retains an honorable place in European pacifist literature. . . . The poems in his *Hymns* . . . voice a humanist's protest against the debasement of man, a victim of powerful states and social systems. They can be likened to the woodcuts of a Flemish rebel against war and oppression, Frans Masereel, one of the most eminent representatives of expressionism in European art. As such, they hold a position of their own, even if Polish poetry veered toward the greater formal discipline of "Skamander" and the First Vanguard.[8]

Julian Krzyżanowski's book is not the only one in which the "figure of silence," as I like to call it, is applied to some eminent Polish poets and writers simply because they did not return to Poland or happened to be still alive in exile. Of dead émigré writers Polish scholars and critics write with more understanding and less restraint. One could list many books and articles, including those that discuss Polish letters abroad, which simply omit many well-known names.[9] It is, therefore, not only desirable but even imperative, that many more books and essays on Polish writers living and writing abroad should appear *outside* Poland, beyond the bounds of Party controls.

Not being an adherent of the biographical approach to poets and writers—with some notable exceptions such as Aleksandr Blok in Russian poetry or Goethe in German letters, I shall confine myself to only those few particular facts of Wittlin's biography which may afford the foreign reader a deeper insight into the workings of his mind and creativity.

Joseph Wittlin was born on August 17, 1896 in Dmytrów, Poland, near the border between the Russian and the Austro-Hungarian Empires to which different parts of Poland had belonged since the Partitions of the country in 1772-1795. He spent his "melancholy" childhood, as he has referred to it more than once, partly in Podolia, in the country, and partly in Lwów, which he considers almost as his native city. He lost his mother at the age of seven. His father remarried two years later and died only six years later when Joseph was barely sixteen. His maternal aunt attempted, at least partially, to take the place of his angelic, beautiful, music-loving mother. His stepmother was an actress, and even now Wittlin remembers her trunks, full of splendid costumes and props, as well as the lessons in drama and poetry reading she gave to the young people.

As a boy Wittlin was high-strung and physically feeble, and by applying a modicum of psychological insight it is easy to account for the fact that such a delicate boy delighted in playing "at being the Japanese General Nogi" during the Russo-Japanese War in 1905.[10] To the author of this book, however, it has been even more enlightening to learn from Dr. Halina Wittlin, the writer's wife, that as a boy he engaged in "forbidden games"[11] on his uncle's estate, burying with much pomp chickens which had been secretly killed by his older cousins. Was he already trying at

such an early age (this must have been before he was ten) to
solve the mystery of death, a problem which was to attract him
unceasingly throughout his work and life? For no one who is
familiar with Wittlin's work can doubt that it is Death and the
dead which have always most fascinated Wittlin, and he succeeded at an early stage in becoming intimate with them. This
fascination is evidenced unusually fully in one of his essays
entitled "Posthumous Works"[12] in which he calls the illumination
of the mysteries of the dead and hell one of the poet's most important tasks. A complete fidelity to this Death motif, which
assumes different disguises (those of the Devil and of War for
example, continues throughout his life, for all its many incon-
sistencies and even paradoxes. And this loyalty helps to explain
at least some of the latter. Thus one can better understand why
the young Wittlin, who had humanist inclinations even in his
early childhood[13] volunteered for the Polish Eastern Legion
which was formed in 1914. Brought up on Polish patriotic mystical song and poetry, and imbued with the ideal of the struggle
to liberate Poland at all costs if only for the sake of those who
had already given their lives in that struggle, he regarded this
war as one decreed "from beyond the grave" and thus "justifiable
and justified."[14] And does not the same fascination with the face
of Death and its transformations account for another irrational
decision that had a major impact on Wittlin's later life and work,
i.e. his joining the Austro-Hungarian Army as a volunteer?

In Wittlin's childhood, the mystique of suffering and of the
wooing of death, themes which have meant much to him both as
man and writer, were already to be found in the works of various
schools of the Symbolist movement. But it was his own early life
experience as well as literary influences, which fostered his predilection for Death and suffering. His rather sad childhood
which included attending school where some of the teachers
were sadists, may explain certain neurasthenic inclinations and
his characteristically pessimistic outlook on life. In an essay in
his *Orpheus*[15] he describes one of his teachers—an old man who
was a sadist, an alcoholic and, to crown it all, a cripple. This
educational misfit mistreated the children beating them regularly
with a big cane. He acquired a new stick each month at his own
expense: ". . . so much did he love thrashing."[16] Naturally such a
school bred phobias and neurasthenia, and could give a sensitive

child like the young Józef a permanently distorted view of life.

In the sixth grade of the Gymnasium he was left a year behind his classmates, proving once more the maxim that talented people are often indifferent to scholastic achievements! Should one trust completely even such a writer as Józef Wittlin, whose autobiographical utterances are remarkably free of any signs of smugness, "self-complacency" or other forms of "self-beautification" and "self-stylization" for the sake of the readers? Should one rely on a poet's reminiscences, or his memory, something which Wittlin himself calls a "falsifier?" This writer has been able to find only one discrepancy in Wittlin's autobiographical reminiscences. In an autobiography, written for *Books Abroad* in 1942, he spoke of his "early maturity,"[17] which he attributed to the three wars he was compelled to witness during his early youth. (He refers to the period between 1914 and 1918, since he regards the Polish-Ukrainian war in Lwów from November 1918 to April 1919 and the Polish-Bolshevik war of 1920[18] as separate wars, not simply as a continuation of the Great War.) But in subsequent interviews with me he has more than once mentioned and bemoaned his late maturity, his inadequate knowledge of so-called "real life," his having lived for too long in the clouds. Of course, the 25-year span that separates these "confessions" may account for the change in his evaluation of his own development, an evaluation which is always most difficult for the person involved.

I *Literary Debut: World War I*

Whether or not he was mature as a person in 1918, he certainly matured and progressed quickly as a poet, translator and writer. Though as a boy he had wanted to become a musician or conductor, his literary triumphs came early. He admits having written melancholy, pathetic poems about graveyards and death at the age of fifteen. He also tried his hand at "tragedies in the style of Wyspianski" and "psychological verse dramas *à la* Ibsen."[19] In 1912 one of his early patriotic poems, "Prologue," a tribute to Zygmunt Krasinski (1812-1859), was published on the occasion of Krasinski's centennial. In that year he also made his first visit to Vienna to attend the funeral of his father who had died there, while seeking treatment in this "medical Mecca" for his illness. And World War I, which followed closely upon Wittlin's literary debut, forced him to complete his Gymnasium

studies not in Lwów but in Vienna, where he later studied at
the University (1914-1916) under such outstanding specialists
in their respective fields as Professor Alois Hoefler (Psychology),
Professor Joseph Klemens Kreibig (Philosophy), Professor Joseph
Strzygowski (Art History) and others. Along with his formal
education went a happy and intensive intellectual life in famous
Viennese cafés, where Wittlin even met Rilke, and where he
was exposed to all the prevailing contemporary currents in literature and the arts. Thus elements from German Expressionism
found their way into his early published work. In Vienna he
met and formed a lifelong friendship with the later eminent
Austrian writer, Joseph Roth (1894-1939). Both volunteered together for the Austro-Hungarian army but were later separated.
The War became one of Wittlin's major themes, perhaps his
main concern and almost an obsession for many years to come.
During the war he matured, lost faith in men, acquired faith in
God, and translated Homer's *Odyssey*, drawing new spiritual
strength from the old classic.

II   *Expressionism*

The war and postwar years are also considered the years of the
emergence of a new literary movement in Poland, known under
the name of Expressionism, which came from the West, Germany and France. Polish Expressionism, especially its Poznan
group *Zdój* (The Spring) has been explored but little. Professor
Julian Krzyżanowski brushes it off in a few scoffing lines of his
History of Polish Literature. It is still being disputed whether
Polish Expressionism dates from before World War I (like German Expressionism) and includes parts of the creative output of
such eminent predecessors of it as Stanisław Wyspianski (1869-
1907) and Tadeusz Micinski (1873-1918), Polish Symbolists, as
Wilhelm Feldman maintains,[20] or is to be brought into direct
connection with the founding of *Zdrój* magazine by Jerzy Hulewicz in October, 1917, as Karol Klein states.[21] It is also contro-
versial whether Polish Expressionism should be more decisively
linked with German Expressionism as K. Klein thinks or be
viewed more as a Polish movement, as Klossowicz would have it.[22]
Many facets of Polish Expressionism are still unexplored and
await further competent investigation. Not pretending to be in a
position to solve these dilemmas, I shall limit myself to a very

brief statement on Polish and German Expressionism only in so far as it is pertinent to the discussion of Wittlin's early work.

In *The Spring*, there are many German names alongside the Polish ones.[23] One also encounters eschatological thought, a characteristic of both German and Polish Expressionism, as well as an abomination of European civilization (before but more especially after World War I), and finally a desire to elevate Man (as a form of Spirit, of course!) as the center of the world, stressing man's ethical aspect, his potentialities for ethical transformation. Klein lists the following sources of Polish Expressionism:

1: The late mystical writings of the great Polish Romantic poet Juliusz Slowacki (1809-1849); 2: German Expressionism; 3: The Polish Romantic Cyprian Kamil Norwid (1821-1883); 4: The Bible. Walter Sokel, in a very interesting study devoted to German Expressionism, sees the words *"O, Mensch!"* ("O, Man!") as one of the leitmotifs of German Expressionism.[24] Compassion and attention to *every* (Italics mine, Z. Y.) human being and a belief in his fundamental goodness pervade the Expressionist writings, both Polish and German, though the Polish Expressionists liked to stress their native roots. Years later Wittlin called Expressionism "a mission in life, a religious and social mission."[25] He saw its failure in its attempt to reform real life by abstract and ultraindividual means, in its having addressed not the real but an abstract reader, and in its proclaiming "other-worldliness" as the only worthwhile domain.

The Polish Expressionists—Adam Bederski, Jerzy and Witold Hulewicz, Zenon Kosidowski, Emil Zegadlowicz and Jan Stur, one of their principal theoreticians—called themselves a "metaphysical movement"[26] and proclaimed in the tradition of Slowacki an absolute supremacy of the Spirit over the Body. We read in their manifesto "What do we want" (Czego chcemy) that everything originates in the Spirit. At the same time we discover their spiritual provenance—the Polish Romantics and Neo-Romantics, i.e. the Polish Symbolists.[27] It is noteworthy that it was one of the Polish Symbolists (the movement known primarily by the name of "Mloda Polska"—Young Poland), Stanislaw Przybyszewski (1868-1927), who wrote extensively about Expressionism in *The Spring*, connecting it with Polish Romanticism[28] and especially with the mystical writings of Juliusz Slowacki.

(In an interview with me Wittlin called Przybyszewski a "John the Baptist" of Polish Expressionism.) Przybyszewski quoted Slowacki at length in a tract entitled "Ekspresjonizm, Slowacki i Genezis z Ducha" ("Expressionism, Slowacki and the Genesis from the Spirit"),[29] maintaining that Expressionism was seeking to answer the eternal tragic questions of humanity: What is birth and rebirth? What are life and death? Przybyszewski defines art as a *"creative realization"* (Przybyszewski's italics) "of the state of the human soul when the lower soul is extinguished and the Pneuma-Spirit is liberated and takes over."[30]

The Expressionists' aim was, according to Przybyszewski and other Expressionists, to liberate oneself from the "yoke of matter" (Przybyszewski's expression). The Expressionists strove to express the pure spirit, freed from all unnecessary material influence. Since everything material is considered only the form of the spirit, the spirit should always be allowed to find new means of expressing itself and the poet must be ready to sacrifice Beauty for the sake of Truth. And the expression of the subconscious would reveal God, Spirit, and Truth in the human being.[31] Thus Expressionism has often been referred to as "an art of the subconscious, of irrationalism and the metapsyche."[32] Klein gives us this felicitous formulation of Expressionism: "Expressionism is an objectivization of a psychic tension and of the visions which impress themselves upon a human being who is in an acute emotional state . . . when the power of mind is partially suspended, finally in the state of half-dream and half-awakening, in the so called hypnoidal states which are prototypes of Expressionistic visions, of that inner vision, upon whose transformation and reflection Expressionism is based.[33] "This explains the often-criticized Expressionists' predilection for exaggeration and distortion of reality: what mattered to them was the soul.[34] Their exaggerations may also have been due to the desire of both Polish and German Expressionists to cry out their feelings and emotions as loudly and directly as possible rather than speaking in more subdued tones. To reproduce their emotions faithfully and impress them upon their readers was their avowed goal. Where words did not suffice, sounds or "music" were used to create the desired effect. Klein mentions the close approximation of the poetry in form to abstract, non-conceptual music and speaks of a "cult of pure sounds in poetry."[35] Characteristically

Jan Stur, in reviewing Wittlin's *Hymns*, praised the "music" and melodiousness of his verse. He called it a "part of the disharmonious harmony of the Universal Spirit."[36]

III   Hymns, *Part I*

It has been said that the introduction of religious, ethical and metaphysical motives by the Expressionists called for large compositional forms like miracle plays, hymns, rhapsodies, etc.[37] The *Hymns* were written by Wittlin during the siege of Lwów in March-October 1918. Having just returned from the Austro-Hungarian army to his native region, Wittlin found Lwów torn by a fratricidal war: first it was besieged by the Ukrainians and then taken over by the Poles. Thus *Hymns* reflect the author's metaphysical longing, his preoccupation with suffering humanity, his protest against war. Many years later, in an important essay entitled "From the Reminiscences of an Ex-Pacifist" (Ze wspomnien bylego pacyfisty), Wittlin sketched out the genesis of his *Hymns*. This essay is worth quoting from here:

> During these long months of bitter struggle poetry was my only salvation from despair. I can confess without any exaggeration that I would have gone mad had I not experienced the grace of poetry. . . . In this most concrete of all worlds, the world of imagination, I have found my truth, my home, my fatherland. At this time, yielding to inner demands, I wrote "Hymn to Hatred," "Lullaby," "The Fear of Death," "Hymn to a Spoonful of Soup," "Longing for a Friend," and "Burying an Enemy." The "content" of these works I drew strictly from reality, not in order to pay tribute to reality, however, but in order to conquer and annihilate this monstrous, ignominious reality by means of poetry.[38]

Traditionally, the hymn is defined as "a laudatory solemn song" or "song of praise" and has been considered a suitable form for expressing religious fervor in a time of spiritual crisis. It has been used by the Church, especially in monastic life, and also to combat heresies and to praise God. Latin hymns, especially the *Dies Irae* which Wittlin often heard at funerals, as well as Polish religious songs, might have influenced the poet to choose this genre at a time of crisis in his life, although in his selection he had an immediate predecessor in the Polish Symbolist poet Jan Kasprowicz (1860-1926). Kasprowicz published his collection of *Hymns*

in two parts in 1898-1901. It was acclaimed by the leading contemporary critics and poets as the summit of his poetry, powerful
in its philosophical and religious implications, its poetic vision
and cosmic dimensions. The first part of Kasprowicz's *Hymns*
which was saturated with eschatological thought, was addressed
"To the Perishing World." The second part, entitled *"Salve Regina,"* revealed a reconciliation with Christian faith and an adoration of Christian ideas and experiences. The noted Polish critic
Jan Józef Lipski argues quite persuasively that Kasprowicz's
Hymns contain many Expressionistic features and that their
author may be considered a predecessor of Polish Expressionism.[39]
Lipski points out the psychological elements in Kasprowicz's
imagery, stresses the role of exaggeration in his style and the
importance here of dichotomy between spirit and matter, which,
in a way also characteristic of the Expressionists, plays an important part in the writer's poetic vision. Finally, Lipski sees
Kasprowicz as a precursor of the eschatological emphasis so
popular with the Expressionists. Lipski's hypothesis seems plausi-
ble, all the more so if one compares Kasprowicz's *Hymns* with
Wittlin's who voiced the same concern for a world now almost
destroyed by the Great War. Wittlin's visions are more concrete,
but no less intense in their emotional impact.

To paraphrase poetry is a difficult and ungrateful task. However, if we are to afford the foreign reader a real insight into the
spiritual-creative world of the author of the *Hymns,* we must
resort to this device. We must begin by stating that they are
pervaded with a sense of metaphysical longing, and intense personal experience: they read more like prayers than poems and
they were so read by Wittlin's contemporaries. The *Hymns* are
not devoid, however, of doubts and contradictions, even blasphemy. Their main theme is war, which forms a general background against which the above-mentioned feelings are dynami-
cally developed. War and Death are great tryers of the spirit.
Wittlin's *Hymns* appeal for peace and for mankind to abandon
their weapons. The author calls for repentance and a return to
faith in God, thereafter a new future for mankind. Some of his
hymns reflect the spirit of a crusader (the crusaders, after all,
did sing hymns!) and of a penitent, rebellious, sinful, and yet
blissful poet-prophet, who has experienced God's grace upon
himself and his lyre, and would like to see others converted to

the faith he has been granted. Wittlin was called—very fittingly—
"a muezzin of his generation."[40]

The tone of the *Hymns* ranges from one of despair, rebellion
and blasphemy to that of psalmodic serenity and Christian humility: Wittlin composed them during walks on the outskirts of
his beloved Lwów, half-singing, half-reciting them aloud. Yet he
succeeds in harmonizing all these dissonant tones into an impressive and very musical whole. The change from a distracted
cry to a quiet, intimate tone, almost that of a whisper, is reflected
in the arrangement of Part I of the *Hymns* in their final form, in
the 3rd edition of 1929.[41]

The book is divided into three parts. In Part I a young and
immature poet, unable and unwilling to restrain himself, cries
out his feelings. Through his voice "all Europe complains" and
even "a mankind of slaves" raises its fists heavenward. He is
representative not only of his own generation but of the entire
human race, which had endured the hell of war. As though gasp-
ing for breath, he says, in "Prelude":

> Within my lungs, gas, dust, the world ablaze
> Still strangle each word that forms in my throat . . .
> Today is purgatory—yesterday was hell;
> Endure, my friends, till evening endure.
> Tomorrow Eden comes into being.
>   *(Translated by Dorothy Meller)*

The poet's *persona* is that of an ex-soldier. In this case the lyrical
mask is reinforced by the facts of Wittlin's own experience. The
soldier is happy to have returned home safe and proclaims, if
half-heartedly, the dawning of a new era: "Manna is falling, and
refreshing dew./Life, bitter, sweetens again." *(Translated by D.
Meller.)* The reference to Biblical manna in a modern context has
a somewhat ironic effect. The same motif will be later used by
Wittlin in the chilling poem "To the Jews in Poland," written in
1942. This little touch of irony widens and deepens as Part I of
the *Hymns* progresses. The sense of horror and ruin which is the
after-effect of the "world ablaze" invests the scenes and images
of the succeeding hymns with authentic life.

The "Hymn of Hatred" presents a succession of dynamic and
dramatic pictures (an Expressionist trait) in which Hatred (an

allegorical figure) assumes various forms, acting as the principal
dramatis persona. It takes the shape of a streetwalker, who casts
spells which make the holy images in churches "grow pale,"
changes good black soil into sand and lifegiving water into the
sewage of big cities, turns children into criminals, peasants into
murderers, and returning soldiers into plunderers and pyro-
maniacs. These scenes, which chase after each other in rapid
succession and startle the reader by the plasticity of the metamorphoses, culminate in the colossal picture of a murderous
danse macabre, in which the Harlot Hatred, breaking into a wild
dance, poisons the peasants with alcohol, plays a tune, beats
time and impels the peasants and their masters to murder each
other: "And peasants and lords cut each others' throats. . . ." The
allegory, an offshoot of Wittlin's observations of the street-
walkers, walking arm-in-arm with officers of the victorious armies
in Lwów, is not merely a rhetorical device; it is also a vehicle
for the young poet's abhorrence, sorrow and disgust.

The "Hymn of Hatred" is followed by "The Fear of Death,"
stressing the unsavory naturalistic details which the Expressionists
reveled in when expressing their negative attitude to the ma-
terialistic side of life. The fear of death drives the poet to utter a
blasphemy. (In Wittlin's opinion blasphemy is one of the ways
of communicating with God.) He calls God "Our most beautiful
invention" and our "False Father." However, immediately after-
wards he assumes—like Kasprowicz before him—the role of a new
Adam, and a new Abraham, father of all righteous men, and like
Abraham he asks God to forgive our sins, if he finds but one
righteous man. After the blasphemy comes a supplication, revealing the insecurity and sadness of the human condition and
the hope of one who passionately believes in God's ultimate mercy.

"The Hymn to a Spoonful of Soup"[42] describes in simple, una-
dorned, but poignant diction the wretched plight of a foot soldier
doomed to perish who has asked for a spoonful of hot soup,
which the poet would have liked to give to him, but it was already
too late. Wittlin has explained that the spoonful of soup was not
meant symbolically, but quite literally.[43] Here the cry of a dying
soldier has the genuine ring of thirst and exhaustion, and the
author's compassion, his genuine concern for the least of human
beings, comes fully to light. "O, Man!" may be considered one of
the leitmotifs of his poetry as well. Why did the soldier have to

fall in this senseless war? Perhaps God will reveal the answer to him after his death. . . . The poet is not afraid to ask God even more direct questions than this; he is not afraid to blaspheme. An ironic reply to the question of why the simple foot soldier had to perish is given in the next hymn, "Burying an Enemy," where Wittlin says:

> And you are lying in the field that is fallow
> For you were told to go to war by the chiefs,
> And they were told by the kings,
> And the kings were told by their pride and by God.
> All power comes from God,
> He puts kings upon the thrones,
> That is why you are lying dead.
>
> *(My translation, Z. Y.)*

The author of the hymn was told to bury an enemy[44] because the design of his cap and buttons are those of the enemy, even though his hand is as hurt and tired as the hand of a brother. The poet has been seized by a sudden sympathy for the unknown soldier. He feels that his heart has been poisoned, and that when the burial is finished he has turned into a stone. A blend of sympathy, grief, abhorrence, irony and scorn is artfully woven together in simple, poignant words and rhythms, which take on the musical structure characteristic of soldiers' songs and funeral marches. There is also a vision of a "peasant paradise," written in quasi-pastoral tones and framed in the characteristic three-line stanzas of Polish church songs, which sums up the essential message, of Wittlin's *Hymns*. It is a paradise in which everyone, people of all nations, "the German, and the Jew, the Roman, the Pole, the Czech, and the Russian" will embrace each other. God will play a song on His pipe,[45] a song which will contain everything—"All wrongs and injuries and all hopes. This sad song will make our souls innocent and holy." Here Wittlin's youthful, utopian faith in the possibility of influencing people through poetry and song is still intact. But Part II of the *Hymns* already shows a waning of this belief.

Two more hymns, "In Praise of the Sword" and "Lullaby" complete Part I of the *Hymns*. "In Praise of the Sword" is satirical in intent and employs the time-honored device of praise-as-blame.

Even its form, the traditional ll-syllable-line alternating with an eight-syllable-line, serves to express irony. Irony surges from below, overlaid by "big" words, archaisms and clichés, but exposed by prosaic touches of bathos. The ancestor's sword, adored by crowds and laid in the cathedral to be offered to the Mother of God, is showed up as a false god and an affront to the sufferings of Jesus Christ and the Mother of God. Irony ranges in this poem from subtle allusions to derision, scorn, sarcasm, and open invective:

> Here is the sword of Damascene steel
> And here is the heart of the Mother of God,
> Pierced through seven times by seven swords,
> And here is the suffering and death of Jesus Christ, spit on.
> *(My translation, Z. Y.)*

In order to make the greatest possible impression upon the reader's sensibilities, Wittlin expresses his pacifism in various forms. In this poem rhetorical devices prevail as his mode of expression.

The last poem of Part I, "The Lullaby" links the beginning and the end of the first cycle of hymns. No longer shouting as in the "Prelude" the poet now addresses his audience directly in a whisper, as the tension mounts:

> I shall whisper into your ear
> A word that beseeches you
> In the Name of the Father and the Son . . .
> "Lay down your arms!"
> *(My translation, Z. Y.)*

Wittlin hopes to reach his reader's *ear:* that secret channel leading into the human soul. One could draw a parallel here to Rilke, whom Wittlin valued highly and translated early, who also regarded the ear as a passage leading to man's inner world.[46] He is at his stylistic best when he whispers, attaining an exquisite fabric of sound and an incantatory tone. These sounds seem to induce the visitation of some holy guests (resembling the Biblical Trinity). He promises peace and a blissful sleep without sensations to the dead ones, and his promises sound like lamentations. . . .

IV Hymns: *Part II*

The "Lullaby" forms an appropriate transition to Part II of the *Hymns* which is devoted to more intimate, but no less explosive emotions. In "Ballad-hymn" the patriotic themes predominant in Polish poetry before Poland's liberation in 1918 are replaced by a more cosmopolitan outlook. "World, you are my Fatherland!" Wittlin exclaims at the end of the poem. The next hymn in Part II is addressed "To the Adversary"; it transfers to the spiritual plane the conflict between the "enemies." There they stand, each in its own zone, like "two great tears, pure and immaculate, that had fallen from God's eyes down into the world, down from high heaven, two living, hot tears, which know nothing of each other." During the daytime they fight, but at night they are both sad because they realize that they are both struggling for the same "unique, unnamed and Holy Thing."

Next comes "A Hymn of Restlessness, Madness and Boredom," which gives poignant expression to the author's feelings of nausea, restlessness, and boredom. Although written 15 or more years before Sartre's celebrated *La Nausée* (1936), it already has an existentialist ring. The emotional intensity of the hymn is fully Expressionistic and the author's emotions are clad in plastic and dynamic images. He does not want to accept the world around him, he searches for its *raison d'être,* for a solution to his longings and his thoughts, only to find that there is no limit to either. He tries to seize the moment when the miracle he has waited for since childhood would occur. But in vain: the happiness for whose sake he has "learned how to think and speak" eludes him. There is no end to the anguish caused by his longings, no stilling of all the unknown forces which slumber in his body and soul or . . . "in thy soul, whosoever thou art." Thus it is not only "I," but "thou" and "we" that concern the poet. He suffers under "the yoke of matter" (to use Przybyszewski's phrase), from the immutability and passivity of the material things which surround him. His feelings aspire to regain a universal meaning. His soul (one of the key words of the German and Polish Expressionists) and his body long first for movement, and then for stillness and rest. He wishes he had a different head, different eyes and ears and completely different perceptions. He would like "to get right out of . . . himself." His blood is complaining and howling, in-

sistently demanding new rhythms! Now the storm rages throughout the domain of his soul: Wittlin, a master of extended metaphors and similes, depicts this outburst brilliantly:

> All five senses are turned loose into madness
> Orgies on a rampage in every dark corner of every blood cell
> Alas, alas!
>> *(Translated by Valerie Hollander)*

The author of the hymn, the lyrical "I," lapses into madness:
he wants to be fed through his nose, to sing with his legs (Wittlin
is very sensitive to gestures and has an unerring eye for their
hidden meaning: they "sing" to him . . .), to speak with his hands
and leave his eyes for kissing. He lapses into a swing . . .

> to the left and to the right,
> to the left and to the right

and then will

> walk back and forth at the same time
> back and forth at the same time!

This reminds one of Gogol's madman from "A Madman's Diary,"
who changes into the Spanish king in order "to step out of himself." Part 3 of this hymn seems to confirm the parallel:

> The whole earth is yawning now—
> From the sewers of the earth
> A stench spreads—[47]
>> *(My translation, Z. Y.)*

thus closing with a vision of cosmic boredom (Gogol was the
first in Russian literature, to my knowledge, to describe this
feeling of boredom. It has been called by Vsevolod Setchkarev
Gogol's "Existential ennui."[48]) The end of the hymn sounds quite
modern in this respect:

> People are yawning prolongedly,
> Their souls are biting their nails,
> The trees are yawning in the gardens,

> The Alps and the Tatra mountains are bored—
> The depths of all oceans are grumbling
> With senile weariness
> And even the wind, that madman,
> has hidden his whirls in a box
> and is yawning in every chimney.
> . . . the eyes of lovers are yawning,
> the senses, desires are yawning,
> so are all raptures,
> all fervors—even the wings
> of all the shiny eagles . . .
> The universe is gaping its jaws—
> is lolling thousands of tongues . . .
> and yawning.
> Uaaaaaaaaaaa—————!
>
> *(My translation, Z. Y.)*

This mood of hopelessness and restlessness persists also in the "Hymn of Fire" where the poet asks God to extinguish him like a holy fire, like a lamp which has been burning too long. He does not want to burn any longer, for he has not succeeded in kindling "the hearts of all cities," nor in kindling all the forests or melting the gold hidden in fireproof safes. He would like to die while he is still in the bloom . . . of his flames.

In the "Hymn of Hymns" the poet, representing "God's people" and the crowd in a Whitmanesque way, boldly asks God to "let him in" to God's abode, "to open up," or at least to show Himself from the balcony and answer but one question: "what is my aim?" (See the "Hymn of Restlessness, Madness and Boredom," where the same question is asked.) Further on this question becomes "what is *our* aim" (Italics mine, Z. Y.)—thus spanning Part I and Part II of the *Hymns.* "Open up," otherwise I will be forced to believe that You are not there at all, that You are dead. . . ." This passage, though reminiscent of Nietzsche's famous dictum, sounds curiously modern, especially in the light of the "God-is-dead theology" preached by people like Altizer.

> Let me in! I have come to
> mourn over the dead body of a king,
> of a king and father,
> who was killed by our disbelief!
>
> *(My translation, Z. Y.)*

"No, it cannot be true!" the poet exclaims. God is not dead. He may, however be asleep, "tired of the immensity of fatherhood." He may be dwelling on another planet, "where happiness falls at His feet at every step like leaves. . . ." At the end of the hymn the poet confesses his love for God, Who is Pure Spirit with no body whatsoever, no body which suffers pain as humans do. The finale of the hymn is built round a juxtaposition of "the soul of this hymn," God, and the pain of the one who wrote it. This dichotomy between Body and Spirit was to become one of the predominant themes in Wittlin's works. God as the "soul" of the poet's creation corresponds to the Catholic theology of Divine inspiration, as found in the Scriptures, the Fathers and Scholastics.

Against the background of three hymns full of doubt, torments and metaphysical longings, the "Hymn to Serenity of the Spirit" stands out as a contrast. It is a paean written in continuous *rinforzando* of praise and ecstasy. The poet has "returned to himself" after years of absence, God has "tuned his lyre," has inspired him with a serene and cheerful song. The motif of the visitation of some holy beings, alluded to in the "Lullaby," is taken up again. The poet has himself experienced God's grace and prophesies the same experience for others.

In the "Psalm" Wittlin half-seriously, half-jokingly, assumes once more the stance of a poet-prophet, the usual mask of Romantic and Neo-Romantic poets. He says that God should be praised in all tongues, and with all instruments, for God has infused His own Soul into them. God should be praised by all rivers, including the little nameless ones in the places where Wittlin spent his childhood; for even this rivulet is known to God and accounted for by Him. This praise is frequently based upon contrasts:

> Be Thou praised with all the odors which Thy earth produces
> All corn which the poor want for their bread.
> *(Translated by Adam Gillon)*[49]

A *pointe* closes the hymn: "And be Thou praised with the prayer of those that believe not in Thee."[50]

The "Psalm" is a fitting finale to the main body of the *Hymns*. It is pervaded by the Christian spirit of this modern man, artist and ironist. It shows his continuous inner struggle, his desire to return to the faith of his childhood (he says that he will sing the psalm by means of the remnants of his childhood) and his inability to do so. We cannot doubt the sincerity of his feelings despite their rhetorical form. The juxtaposition of two different kinds of praise, positive and negative (as shown above) produces a powerful and effective tension.

V   *Non-Hymns*

Part III of the *Hymns* contains "Non-Hymns" as a counterpart to the Hymns. It shows the versatility of the young poet, whose lyre is capable of various tones and tunes. "Non-Hymns" point to the future line of Wittlin's development as a poet. In the first poem, "A Mother Bids Farewell to Her Only Child," a dying mother apostrophizes her only son and tries to reconcile herself to her imminent death by thinking of the many children who await her Beyond. However, she cannot tear herself away from her only little one, whose fate, down to the minutest detail, is of the most concern to her: "Who will mend your stockings tomorrow, when I am not here?" She asks God to give her faith in the eternity of the soul, as her one possible consolation. Thus the issues of faith and doubt, despair and serenity of soul, appear in the "Non-Hymns" as well. Three short epigrammatic poems close the volume. "Blanks" shows the poet's dissatisfaction with existing linguistic and artistic methods and devices, especially with worn-out words and rhymes. In this poem he uses blanks (. . .) for those cliché rhymes that everyone will be able to fill in without much thought. Wittlin has battled strenuously against words even slightly suspect of descending into "clichédom" and against the automatic repetition of "empty words" (the title of one of his essays). Some of these worn-out words were laughed out of existence precisely by Wittlin and others who were equally sensitive to the deadening of the living Polish language. Thus Wittlin developed the practice of putting "so-called" in front of every word or phraseological unit that has become worn out by over-usage. There is no end to the ironic effects he achieves in this way in his poems and essays alike. (cf. "In Praise of the Sword" where "so-called" annihilates a pompous cliché like "field of glory," i.e. battlefield, as it used to be called in war accounts and operations orders.)

Two short epigrams which deal with things eternal and essential demonstrate Wittlin's wit at an early stage of development. In one of them he wonders when the spirit, "this excellent dentist," will extract "the tooth of time," which is destroying our nerve tissues and exploiting our labor. It sounds quite modern in the light of all the new theories about time which preoccupy modern scientists. Once more we confront the dichotomy between things temporal and transient and the Spirit, which ought to be victorious in the strife between Spirit and matter, between Jacob and the Angel (a comparison frequently used by Wittlin). We see how irony and wit are gaining ground here, leaving behind the pathos of the *Hymns,* but not their ethos. And irony will come to the fore in *The Salt of the Earth* where the unwritten poetry continues to be felt beneath, lending a peculiar aspect to the prose texture of that work. *The Salt of the Earth* shows how Wittlin's idealism and youthful utopianism has given way to a more skeptical and pessimistic view of life, a view that had been inherent in some poems of The *Hymns* and which will manifest itself more directly in his later poetry, written from 1921-1939.

VI   *On the Structure of the* Hymns

The *Hymns* are oratorical or rhetorical in structure, though they have some narrative and descriptive features as well. It has been said that epic elements are more prevalent in them than lyrical ones[51] but the *Hymns* contain so many emotional elements and lyrical apostrophes, so many "mindscapes," every description in them is so subordinated to the mood of the lyrical "I" that one should consider them as predominantly lyrical. This lyrical "I" is here itself one of the so-called "represented objects" (Roman Ingarden's terminology, cf. his *Das literarische Kunstwerk,* which is now being translated into English). It is closely connected with its surroundings which are colored by its emotions. The world is portrayed in a synthetic way, typical of a lyrical presentation. There are only a few concrete, epic details and these are submerged beneath lyrical vehemence, grandiose poetic visions, symbols and images. Details are often exaggerated, in keeping with the poetics of Expressionism. The *Hymns* are directed to an imaginary audience or to specific individuals (cf. "To the Adversary") with the aim of impressing them, trying to make them share the author's beliefs and even act accordingly (the Expressionists' goal). Wittlin's oratorical style is characterized by frequent parallelisms of various kinds (thematic, syntactic, lexical), by questions, exclamations, exhortations. It is often hyperbolic, saturated with images and similes, rather extended, made dramatic by plastic visions and metamorphoses (as in the "Hymn of Hatred"). The tone changes from lyrical-apostrophic to satirical-sarcastic, the volume from a shriek to a whisper. The unity of the structure is achieved by the unity of the themes which encompass God, War, the human soul after the war and the lyrical "I." This *persona* is an extremely sensitive individual with a vivid imagination, devoted to solving the "eternal cursed questions" (Dostoevsky's phrase) of faith and lack of faith, of the split between Spirit and Body, the dichotomy between life and death.

Unity is also achieved by the composition of the whole. The basic device seems to be a repetition of the main motif or of several motifs which are closely related and it reminds one of a musical composition where a leitmotif appears, disappears and reappears in different variations. The basic motif may be given at the very beginning, in the opening verse *(capoverso)*, as in "Burying an Enemy," where the author says that "his heart is poisoned," and repeated at the very end with a variation, thus framing the whole structure: "In vain am I carrying around my poisoned heart. . . ." It is an instance of *epanalepsis,* though somewhat incomplete. Compositional unity can be achieved by anaphora as in the "Prelude," where four anaphoras in four stanzas out of five build up the dramatic tension, bringing the whole composition to a climax, only to collapse in the final stanza with an abrupt change of tone and meaning, followed by an antithesis at the end which again heightens the tension. In addition, the first three stanzas show a bipartite composition in which recollections of the horrors of war are superseded by a more cheerful "here-and-now":

> Within my lungs gas, dust, the world ablaze,
> Still strangle each word that forms in my throat.
> Oh, how sublime the grace of God
> That I crossed these seas of blood
> To you, kind people.
>
> *(Translated by Dorothy Meller)*

Only the fourth stanza, just before the finale, does not have a bipartite composition; first, there is a crowd of dynamic visions of a "threatening, shouting" postwar Europe, followed by a resolution into the promise of a better future and "sweeter" life.

We have also a bipartite composition in the "Hymn to Serenity of the Spirit," where each two-line stanza consists of a question and an answer. Sometimes Wittlin uses variations of anaphora (as in the "Hymn of Hatred") substituting different words in various stanzas "and" ("a" in Polish), "when" and "as." He particularly likes "and" at the beginning of a stanza, which helps him to couch his hymns quite often in a somewhat Biblical style. One can attribute to this "Biblical" style (especially in the "Hymn of Hatred" and the "Hymn of Hymns") his frequent archaisms and parallelisms. Some other forms of repetition for the sake of achieving unity in composition; i.e. repetitions within structural units, are also used by Wittlin. He is especially fond of leitmotifs, using them with many variations. Thus the "Hymn of Hymns" has four refrains: "Let me in!," "Open up," "Show yourself," "Wake up," which are repeated interchangeably, increasing the tension and heightening the dramatic quality, favorite aims of the Expressionists. These exhortations are emotionally colored and disclose sudden changes in the poet's mood in a way impossible in a shorter poem (this hymn has 188 lines!). Let us remember that frequently refrains have been used as a "binding" device in religious song. In the "Hymn to Restlessness . . ." each of the three parts has its own leitmotif. The diverse material is connected internally by anaphoras. We also have in the "Hymn to Hands" an example of a poem framed by a refrain, "Speak softer," which is also repeated twice inside the composition. This hymn is composed like a piece of music, based upon "pianos" and "fortes," and ringing repetitions with all kinds of variations of the key word "hands," either named directly, or described by means of paraphrase, creating an additional tension:

> Hands, oh, hands, generous hands,
> Hands, oh, hands, industrious hands!
> Hands, you pair of living maledictions! (Forte)
> *(My translation, Z. Y.)*

The hymn contains an intricate interplay of sound patterns, creating the effect of language striving to become music.

Contrast is also used as a compositional device in the *Hymns*. Not only is contrast an appropriate finale to some of the poems (as in the "Hymn of Hymns"), but Wittlin uses contrast within one and the same structural unit (stanza), as in "Psalm." This effectively creates a tension within the stanza.

VII *Vocabulary, Archaization, and Images*

The oratorical style presupposes the choice of solemn words, an archaic syntax, and an extensive use of tropes and figures. Wittlin uses archaic words and archaic syntactic constructions to a moderate degree, combining them for greater expressiveness with everyday and sometimes even vulgar words (cf. "In Praise of the Sword.") There are some dialectisms for the sake of stylization, as in "Burying an Enemy." Wittlin shows great mastery in creating clusters of words around the key words of the poem, thus extending their meaning, reinforcing the texture and making possible smooth transition between the stanzas. Thus in "Hymn of Hymns" the poet's bitter complaints and longing for communion with God, existentialist feeling of *Geworfenheit* (in Heidegger's phrase) are expressed by means of very concrete images of waiting for God's appearance in front of His "palace," or His "gate," "threshold," "sanctuary," "courtyard," "balcony," and "throne." All these words, belonging to similar semantic fields, link the stanzas into an organic whole. In Part II of the same hymn we have bitter complaints about human suffering, which take the form of "wailing," "pain," "grief," and rise in gradation to "heartbreak" and "despair." Human afflictions are extended by metonymy to cities, houses and streets which "suffer," "wail," "bleed" and "expire." The picture is sharpened by the image of the complaints of the living and the dead (!) which are tied up in a sack (Perhaps a classical allusion to a Pandora's box?) and carried by the poet to God. Wittlin also favors extended and developed metaphors which sometimes encompass an entire poem, as in the "Hymn of Fire." Frequent words in the *Hymns* such as "pain," "distress," "agony," "anguish," "sweat," "blood," "corpse," "grave" are projected onto a metaphorical plane and abstract concepts and metaphors are "realized," or materialized, "literalized." In the "Hymn to the Adversary," "struggle" means only a spiritual combat, and "corpse" is applied to "contradictory thoughts": "the corpses of our con-

tradictory thoughts." Of all the various types of metaphor, Wittlin
especially favors and shows unusual skill in using personifications.
He possesses a mythic imagination even though both his precur-
sors Homer and Kasprowicz use a great deal of anthropomorphization as well. Thus Wittlin animates the sword in "In Praise of
the Sword," alluding to those who venerate it as a deity. In his
picture of cosmic boredom in the "Hymn of Restlessness . . ." the
cosmos itself is animated, "lolling thousands of tongues and
yawning." A splendid personification encompassing the entire
poem is presented in "Pain of the Tree," in which the story of the
suffering of a tree which was used as Jesus's Cross, is strikingly
portrayed. Wittlin succeeds in making the tree a deeply feeling
and suffering, intelligible being. More than that—he shows the
intimate emotions of the tree's soul ("trees do have a heart," says
the author parenthetically), its partaking of the sufferings of
Christ relates it to the most human of men. Wittlin universalized
here the wretchedness of mankind. The pain of the tree merges
with the suffering of Christ and the anguish of Wittlin as man
and poet. Suffering makes true communion possible. The cosmic
unity of everything that lives is expressed very convincingly
through a complete anthropomorphization. There are few examples of poets with such a power of empathy *(Einfühlungsver-
mögen)*. The wailing, "the morning anthems of the tree, imbued
with longing," its "perfect weeping," reveal the innermost layer
of the hymn which, as is so often the case in Wittlin's poems, is a
lament. Personifications make Wittlin's poetic world highly
dynamic, expressive and dramatic. Everything comes alive and
acts—not only objects but the most abstract concepts: abstract
words predominate over concrete in the *Hymns*. Blending of the
abstract and the concrete is often achieved by the author, in a
"sudden glory of a fused metaphor."[52] Thus the poet feels "the
hot breath of eternity" ("Hymn to Hands"), a day is "panting"
(heaving), "A phantom of fear walks behind him" ("Hymn to
Hands"), "the complaint shouts" ("Intermezzo"). Wittlin uses
epithets to metaphorize his style; psychological and lyrical epithets color his concrete objects emotionally, or accentuate abstract words. Thus we have: "The *mute* passivity of a chair," or
the "immutability" of a table is termed "horrible" and "dead"
depending upon the author's state of mind, the soul is "hungry,"

blood is "yearning," death is "thirsty" ("Hymn to a Spoonful of Soup").

Wittlin also revitalizes old clichés and stereotypes that have been in use since the days of the Romantics. For example we would be inclined to regard "seas of blood" in the "Prelude" as a stereotyped phrase, if Wittlin did not revitalize its evocative and dynamic power by saying that he "has crossed the seas of blood." The same process holds true of "poisoned heart," another phrase from the Romantic repertoire. Weaving this well-worn metaphor into the plot and texture of his hymn, Wittlin shows *how* the poisoning has taken place. Nor does he use colors in their literal sense but in terms of their symbolic expression. Thus "black" is the color of "mourning," "green" signals something ominous (Hatred has green eyes, a moment looks at Wittlin "with a green eye"; this color may mean the imminent death of someone dear to him). And in general words become symbols of psychological acts; they mark delicate and sometimes turbulent tides and turns of emotion within the poet's soul; they express not only his own spiritual state but potentially that of any man.

Wittlin's poetry is composed like songs where one's attention is focused upon emotions, not upon logical meanings as such. This book is not the place to attempt analysis of the intricate sound pattern of Wittlin's *Hymns* important as that aspect of his poetry undoubtedly is. Unfortunately his sound effects are usually completely lost in translation. Here I shall confine my remarks to a very brief summary of his handling of sounds in conjunction with his use of meter and rhyme.

VIII   *Rhythm, Versification, Sound Effects*

Wittlin uses free verse rhythms—in the appropriately chosen form of hymns with great mastery. His immediate models in the use of free verse were Kasprowicz and Verhaeren. His rhythms convey all the minute fluctuations of emotion, they carry its ebb and flow with great ease. He does not borrow ready-made rhythms; his blood longs for "new rhythms" and he often achieves them. His rhythms are usually appropriate to his subject matter. It has been observed that parts of the "Hymn of Hatred" were written to the "dancing tune of a street song."[53] This is completely in accordance with the central image-allegory of Hatred, which was born out of his reminiscence of a streetwalker in Lwów. The sound pattern reinforces his vision. Similarly, the part of "Burying an Enemy" which immediately follows the peasant's conscription is written in the form of a folk and military song. The peasants' Paradise, depicted in the latter part of the hymn, has the form of a church song, with three lines of an equal number of syllables in each stanza. The stanzas of the *Hymns* are not uniform. Wittlin shows in this a great mastery as well. He likes to use lines of uneven length, which he links together by means of a refrain or a rhyme. Only "In Praise of the Sword" has the regular traditional ll-syllable verse with 5-line stanzas and a variation of 8 syllables in the fifth line. The traditional 8-syllable line reinforces the third line ironically. For the "Hymn to Serenity of the Spirit" Wittlin employs variations of the hexameter, as was noticed perceptively by Kleiner.[54] His rhythmical variability is considerable for so young a poet. Homer proved to be an excellent master for him in this respect and his studies of Polish, European and American literature, especially of Emil Verhaeren and Walt Whitman, who both used free rhythms very effectively, were also helpful.

Wittlin has achieved great expressiveness through his use of sounds and images. The musical nature of the *Hymns* strikes the reader immediately. One notes, for instance, that in them all kinds of musical instruments are mentioned and imitated. In "Burying an Enemy" a military orchestra with trumpets, trombones and kettle-drums is apostrophized and then God himself plays the pipe, and the Saints, especially St. Cecilia, make music. In the "Psalm" Wittlin says that God has infused His own soul into musical instruments. Angelic harps are mentioned in the "Hymn to the Serenity of the Spirit," etc. Since in the "Hymn of Hymns" Wittlin says that the soul of his hymn of praise belongs to God, it is easy to deduce that he looks upon his hymn as a song; i.e., a musical composition, and upon himself as a musical instrument of God!

IX *Significance of the* Hymns

The meaning of Wittlin's *Hymns*—indeed of his poetry as a whole—lies in their religious sense, in the yearning of a hard-pressed soul for happiness and communion with God. We constantly sense the poet's fear that the human soul as a result of World War was deteriorating and reaching the state which was described in an expressionistic way as "man's defection from God," as "the extreme consequence of lack of sympathy."[55] Wittlin was called "a poet of peace and love" by the Polish critic Pawel Hulka-Laskowski who saw in him "a deep spiritual kinship and similarity of experiences" with St. Francis of Assisi.[56] (The cult of St. Francis of Assisi has been maintained in Polish poetry by two important poets: Jan Kasprowicz and Leopold Staff [1878-1957].)

While Poland and its intellectuals were rejoicing in their newly won independence and tasting the joys of a true life, Wittlin showed deep concern over the changed make-up of human beings after the Great War and their ensuing physical and moral collapse. In this respect Wittlin saw further than his contemporaries and was in advance of them, for lamentations over the general decline of the European spirit and culture became a prevalent mood among European intellectuals only later in the 1920's and especially in the 1930's. He was concerned with the essential problems of human existence and the current relationship between mankind and God, one that seemed to him highly unsatisfactory in a time of crisis. In his religious songs he was trying to remind his contemporaries of two of the most important realities in life—God and death—both often forgotten in the humdrum of daily existence. He was trying to arouse their concern.

The *Hymns* exploded like a bomb upon the godless, angry postwar generation, summoning it not to arms but to prayer, repentance and promising salvation and peace. I have heard from several of Wittlin's contemporaries that the *Hymns* were actually recited as prayers, along with real prayers. To speak of the tormenting problems of life and death, of deep religious relationships and of the doubts which pain many a religious soul; above all to speak of these in such a frank and dramatic way was no small accomplishment for so young a poet. And it was a major achievement to be able to express such essential truths and values in the form of a seemingly simple song. Wittlin here showed an early mastery of the rhythmic form usually associated with religious songs. His rhythms expressed the surfacing and eruption of his deepest and strongest emotions—an artistic goal of the Expressionists. Developing beyond the influence of his predecessors—Slowacki, Kasprowicz, Verhaeren, Walt Whitman—he knew how to impress on his poetry the individual stamp

of his own talent. Among the many other new voices in modern
Polish poetry his voice emerged as distinctive. Professor Juliusz
Kleiner, reviewing the *Hymns* for *Gazeta wieczorna* (Evening
Newspaper, in Lwów) wrote that "Wittlin has acquired a high
position among the poets of the younger generation," that he
stands next to Julian Tuwim, Jan Lechon and Kazimierz Wierzynski as "a spokesman of the deep, general human emotions
who is full of love for human beings and for God."[57] Karol Klein
said in the above-mentioned article on Polish Expressionism
that Wittlin was the only one of the Expressionists who knew
how to give powerful utterance "to the soul of the modern man
and to lay bare with a great deal of self-knowledge the tragic
aspect of an individual intertwined with the tragedy of the
epoch."[58]

CHAPTER 2

Occasional Verse

WITTLIN has never stopped writing poetry, but the volume announced under the intriguing title of *Kontrabanda* (Contraband) has not yet been published. He wrote some poetry between the two wars as well as after the Second World War. At the present time he is preparing another volume of his Works (For *Kultura*, the Polish magazine and press in Paris) containing the *Hymns* and his early poetry together with some new poems of recent years. Wittlin has written mostly occasional verse (though we must not forget that Goethe once remarked that all poetry is really "occasional verse"–*Gelegenheitsdichtung*). His style has changed considerably since the early 1920's. It may have been the dazzling poetic technique and healthy earthiness of the Skamander group (some of whom, especially Julian Tuwim and Antoni Slonimski, became his life-long friends), that made him examine his earlier metaphysical poetry, which lacked the external brilliance and concision of the Skamandrites' verse. Their poetry became the dominant poetic tendency in the new, independent Poland which was born out of the subsiding pangs of the Great War, out of the prayers and songs and sacrifices of many generations. The older generation, whose representatives in poetry such as Kasprowicz, Staff, Przybyszewski, Lesmian et al. were then still alive, ceded its place (without a fight) to the new generation of poets: Julian Tuwim, Kazimierz Wierzynski, Antoni Slonimski, Jaroslaw Iwaszkiewicz and Jan Lechon —to name only the five principal poets in a loosely connected group. Although Wittlin made his debut in *The Spring,* not in the *Skamander,* the organ of the Skamandrites, he later (especially during World War II when the Skamandrites in exile made a dramatic comeback to the literary scene) became affiliated with them, publishing in the *Skamander* his poems and essays and

even parts of his novel *The Salt of the Earth*. He once quipped
in his polished speech in honor of Kazimierz Wierzynski (at his
70th birthday celebration at the Plaza Hotel in New York), that
"whenever muddy water was poured over the Skamandrites and
blows were distributed, he was counted as one of them; but
whenever praise was lavished upon them, he was, curiously
enough, excluded from their number. . . ." The truth is that in
spirit he has never been a Skamandrite. They had a Dionysian,
passionate approach to the new-found life in the new-born Poland, or at least they had such an attitude for some time, whereas
he had a pessimistic outlook on the world, notwithstanding the
fortunate outcome of that war for his homeland. However, Wittlin admits to being impressed by the Skamandrites as craftsmen
and virtuosi of verse technique. His moving from Lwów, where
he represented the Poznan *Spring* and in other respects lived as
an "independent spirit," first to Lódz (in 1922) where he became
a literary director of the Municipal Theater and a cofounder of
the Dramatic School, then to Warsaw (in 1927), where he was
obliged to engage in literary work professionally, writing and
translating, changed Wittlin as a poet and, perhaps, even im-
pelled his switch to prose. In any case the appearance of his new
poetic style coincided with his move to Warsaw, where he did not
feel quite at home and was not so self-confident. *The Spring*
ceased publication in 1922, the *Skamander* continued until 1928,
and was revived in the 1930's continuing until the outbreak of
war in 1939. Wittlin's association with *Skamander* was viewed in
various ways. A Polish poet of a younger generation, Waclaw
Iwaniuk, once remarked to Wittlin that it was not productive
and that it had prevented Wittlin from becoming "a Polish T. S.
Eliot."

One notices the gap separating the Wittlin of the *Hymns* and
the Wittlin of a later period. As early as 1921, in the "Elegy to
Homer" written to commemorate the completion of his translation
of the *Odyssey I*, he refers to World War I, a cause of so many
powerfully erupting emotions in the *Hymns*, as *"some horrible
war."* (Italics mine, Z. Y.)

I   *Poems of 1921-1939*

Among the poems written between 1921 and 1939, reprinted
in Lam's Anthology[1] and originally published in such Polish

periodicals as *Skamander* we find various genres: two elegies; a ("lowered") ode ("An Ode in Honor of the Polish Language and Polish Poetry"); a "Christmas-Eve-Song on Adam Mickiewicz"; several invectives; a "Litany," "A Funeral Rhapsody in Honor of Stefan Zeromski," "An Epitaph for Aristide Briand," "Knell for a Condemned Man," and the beautiful "Lament XX," written for Jan Kochanowski, the great sixteenth-century poet, and his little daughter (who had died at the age of three). The representative selection which Wittlin made for Lam's Anthology closes with a charming lullaby to his own daughter.

An interesting parallel—showing Wittlin's development as a poet from the early period of the *Hymns* to the prewar period of the late 1930's—can be made by a comparing in detail two poems which have the same title: "Lullaby." Comparing the earlier and later of the two poems we note how Wittlin's poetry becomes more "earthly," more saturated with images and even colors— which are no longer symbolic, but descriptive of the color of real objects. However, we also note that he is still deeply concerned over the bitterness of everything sweet (cf. "Prelude" and "Lullaby for My Baby Daughter" in the Appendix to this book) and with the suffering of humans and animals alike. In his "Lullaby for My Baby Daughter" he wants not only to rock his baby to sleep, but to protect her from all the evil and pain in the world. There are more concrete words in the second Lullaby, and more evocative descriptions and images than abstractions and allegories. Unlike the first, it does not sound like a rhythmic incantation, but like a real lullaby, even to the point of imitating baby talk in its intricate interplay of alliterations and keeping up a "rocking" rhythm.

"Elegy to Homer" is a tribute to the ancient bard by a humble disciple and proud translator who was "chained" to his translating task for seven years. Wittlin uses a leitmotif with variations to connect his stanzas of various length and to achieve unity. Appropriate to the occasion and to the classical genre of elegy are the archaic words with which this poem sparkles. Another elegy, on the theme of his wife's eyes, is built upon the juxtaposition—a device he uses frequently—between the evil eyes of the public which "nail him to the wall like a poster" and the faithful eyes of his beloved wife which burn like two bright lanterns and which he unexpectedly compares to two faithful dogs (in Wittlin's poetry and prose alike the dog often serves as a vehicle in his metaphors and similes). He bares the device in *The Salt of the Earth* where it is written with self-irony: "In due course the dog, an infinitely adaptable metaphor, passed into the stationmaster's vocabulary, and became the most treasured item of all his collection" (p. 137).

The poems dealing with death are highly effective. "Lament XX" illustrates especially well the amazing empathy characteristic of this modern poet in his attempt to show the strength of eternal emotions first voiced by his great predecessor almost four centuries earlier.[2] As usual, whenever human suffering is involved, Wittlin's sensitivity penetrates into its reality enabling him to share another's special variety of pain. "Lament XX" is more than just another lament by a bereaved father; it is the "complaynte" (to cite the sixteenth-century British poetic phrase) of a poet who cannot forget his art even in the moment of his greatest grief and yet who finds no solace in the literary artifices and Stoic philosophy of classical antiquity. He would rather, says Wittlin, cry with real human tears than compose an elaborate and literarily sophisticated lament—a complaint which might also be made by many other poets.

One finds yet another trace of Wittlin's long association with Homer in the unusual and original *sui generis* hexameters of his "Funeral Rhapsody in Honor of Stefan Zeromski" although Wittlin's model for this was probably the famous "Funeral Rhapsody in Memory of General Bem" written by the late Romantic Cyprian Kamil Norwid, whom Wittlin admired and valued highly as a philosophical poet and precursor of modern Polish poetry. Wittlin's "Funeral Rhapsody" is interspersed with allusions to Zeromski's popular works and with archaisms which Zeromski had been fond of using. Wittlin's hexameters are suggestive and appropriate since Zeromski had already used some variations of them in his rhythmical prose, making a deep impression upon his contemporaries and thereby helping to shape the further evolution of Polish prose. Wittlin's rhetorical exclamations and stylization of the funeral procession as a process of floating toward eternity are impressive, as is the comparison of the Polish language to a wailing widow and the final simile in which the poet's voice is said to be lowered like a flag shot through with bullets.

In reviewing Wittlin's total creative output between 1921 and

1939, one cannot but voice one regretful question: why did he write so little poetry during this period? His long "Litany," written in 1937, may help us answer this question at least in part. In this "Litany" Wittlin confesses to God his sin of having remained silent about all the unseemly things which he has witnessed in life. He has kept silent about the debasement of his fellow men, about hunger, about the poverty of the Polish peasants, and about "the wars which are being fought" and those "which will break out." He is silent about the "nightmares" he experiences and only his soul is "shouting silently. . . ." (Allusions to lowered voice, whispering and silence which shouts recur throughout Wittlin's work, bridging the *Hymns*—cf. "Lullaby"—and his other poetry.) He is silent about the Devil who walks about in this world. He asks God not to punish him too severely for his all-embracing silence which has converted his conscience into a dirty and bloody wound. The poem is composed like a litany with only an occasional rhyme to reinforce a particular point (i.e., he rhymes "Madryt"—Madrid and "iperyt"—mustard gas) and with many anaphorae—"I am silent" (cf. translation of the "Litany" in Appendix to this book), but it is really an invective in disguise. The sharp satirical edge is even more prominent here than in those hymns which contain some satirical elements. Two more invectives show the direction in which Wittlin had evolved. They are both directed, as is the "Litany" against the poisoning of the contemporary world by two horrible products of so-called "civilization"; the newspaper (cf. his poem "People in the Streetcar"—see Appendix) and gas, which Wittlin gloomily expected would be used in future wars.

In "The Newspaper" linotype is called "the archenemy," "the Satan" of Europe. It changes blood into ink (a recurrent image with Wittlin) thereby poisoning human lives. It negates the Christian doctrine: "Daily News spits into the face of the Spirit," Wittlin exclaims. The poet who, like a Biblical Noah with his ark, seeks refuge from the newspaper at God's feet, is followed even there by a reporter who wants to open a branch office of the newspaper in heaven and who would like to reduce "the Creation of the World to the level of a newspaper editorial." Here Wittlin's irony cuts deep and glitters with many vibrations. An extended metaphor presents a fitting finale to this invective: God should forbid the Devil to use our pure souls as "spoilage" by putting an end to the world and blotting out "our entire printing and circulation." Thus the eschatological theme, which was so dear to Wittlin, and of which he was an early exponent in what came to be known as the "school of catastrophism" in Polish poetry, is introduced at the slightest provocation. In this poem Wittlin's sarcasm reaches an almost aphoristical concision. The device of contrast heightens and reinforces this invective from beginning to end. There are images and poetic "short cuts" of thought which might have served as stimuli for many new poems had they been less sarcastic. At least one metaphor, however—"sheets of newspapers like shrouds that stink with human suffering"— recurs later as a powerful symbol and a new myth of our forlorn humanity when, in the poem "To the Jews of Poland" (1942), Wittlin says the Jews are wrapped in paper—"the dirty wings of the new Angel of Death."[3]

The second invective, entitled "From Song to the Music of the Future," gives us a vision of the complete destruction of the civilized world in a future war, especially by means of gas. Gas is pictured as a new Moses, a new savior who will reconcile the feuding nations. . . .! Wittlin sees deserts in place of the "mad capitals" of our world, he sees a Sahara where his beloved Place de la Concorde had stood in Paris and only "lonely shadows" walking along the Champs Elysées. Not only the utopian hopes of his early period, but all his hopes of any kind were quickly disappearing in the stifling atmosphere of the prewar period. Only occasionally was Wittlin able to prove once again that his lyre was fit for more than one tune. A beautiful "Ode in Honor of the Polish Language and Polish Poetry" (1937) epitomizes his love and understanding of his native tongue, including its most insignificant parts of speech such as pronouns and adverbs, down to every last feature in the alphabet and even the dots over the "ż"! Here he "lowers" the style of the ode and yet preserves some of the genre's essential features. He praises "everyday words," "worn like old coins" until they are transformed by the "loving hand of the poet" and burst into sacred flame like the "burning bush" (again a Biblical image). Wittlin calls poetic and unpoetic words alike "sinless thieves of the heavenly fire." A quotation from Mickiewicz's *Konrad Wallenrod* about the song that will survive everything on earth closes the ode.

Another "occasional verse," dedicated to the Polish artist Tola

Korian, now residing in Chicago, entitled *A la Recherche du Temps Perdu,* affords an insight into Wittlin's development as a poet. His poetic "via" grew steadily narrower as he searched for the utmost economy of artistic expression, and by the same token became tired of all the available words and sought to defamiliarize poetic vision and poetic diction, and tended more and more toward aphoristic formulations. The poem is quoted here in its entirety, as it provides a good example of Wittlin as a thoroughly modern and modernistic poet, with an eye for the incongruous, the ironical and the grotesque, discovering existential depths beneath the surface of the most routine and everyday phenomena. The poem, like other poems of this period, affords an example of a perfect blending of "high" and "lofty" words with ordinary ones—including vulgarisms—into an artistically satisfying whole for which technique credit must be given to the *Skamander* school as a whole.

A la recherche du temps perdu
For Tola Korjan

I, Anna Csillag of the luxuriant hair,
Smiling sweetly, ever the same,
Have for thirty years reigned over the columns
Of your newspapers, as though a saint.

I hold a spray of stars as though it were a lily.
Time does not alter my angelic beauty:
Downy carpet of unfastened hair
Boisterously cascades down to my feet,
To the bare feet of the goddess of hair.

I, Anna Csillag, throughout thirty years,
Have known neither sorrow nor pain;
But, what happened to you, my son:
You look at me and you are weeping?

As for me, Anna Csillag—even during those years
When your brothers' blood had stained half the world,
And printer's ink was saturated with blood,
And death shouted at me from adjacent columns—
Not one of my hairs turned gray,
Not a hair of my head was lost.

O Anna Csillag, the holy newspaper image
Of our bygone youthful days:
I walk about the world and gather rubbish—
Soon I'll become a relic of myself.

And I shall write even duller verses
A la recherche, à la recherche
Du temps perdu.

(Translated by Dorothy Meller)

Anna Csillag,[4] a "newspaper saint," a goddess for growing one's hair, according to a popular prewar advertisement for a Polish "elixir" for growing hair, is still adored by many readers of the ever-increasing mass of newspapers and popular magazines. She may have changed her outer appearance with the growing sophistication of Madison Avenue, but she is still "smiling sweetly." The aphoristic and self-ironizing phrase "soon I'll become a relic of myself" makes a fitting end to this poem and to other poems in this group full of inverted images of "ultimate things" and ironic projections of "eternal questions," and full too, of self-irony and an almost parodistic presentation of the poet's own feelings. The condensed images and compacted irony here show in Wittlin a mature master; indeed, his poems of the 1930's have a craftsmanlike quality which had previously been absent. A closer look at Wittlin's imagery discloses many Biblical and mythological reminiscences and motifs such as predominate throughout Wittlin's poetry, including his "New Poems" of the 1960's.

"Land of Milk and Honey," "Messiah," "Noah," Judas, Jericho, Eve, Cain, cherubs, angels, devils, "the bitter cup," "manna," "hell," "the fiery sword," "the burning bush," and other such Biblical matter can be found in Wittlin's poetry from the *Hymns* right through to "New Poems." However Wittlin uses them for the most part not in their traditional sense, but for his own purposes, often even attaining grotesque effects as in the poem "Newspaper" where the newspaper shouts like "the hoarse trumpets of Jericho," or in the invective "From the Song to the Music of the Future" where gas is referred to as a "Savior" and "Messiah." An interesting example of a "realized metaphor," a metaphor whose figurative meaning is replaced with a literal one (practised by Wittlin also in prose) is provided by one of the "New Poems," "Lament of a Sacrificial Ram" where it forms the whole poem. Wittlin, who is not especially inventive as regards plot, uses the device of "realization of the metaphor" or "literalization" to advance the "plot," as we shall see in *The Salt of the Earth*.

Mythological reminiscences are often implied rather than stated openly, while a periphrasis tends to create an additional tension: thus in the "Ode in Honor of the Polish Language and Polish Poetry" words are referred to first as "winged chargers of the royal stud" (cf. Dorothy Meller's translation in the Appendix) i.e., Pegasuses, and then are called "sinless, benevolent thieves of fire divine"—i.e., Prometheuses. Wittlin's mythic imagination of *Beseeltypus*[5] makes everything alive, especially words which are rendered "ablaze, holy, like Sinai's bush" (in the same poem) under the "Poet's loving hand," or they trail (literally *drag*) on their knees behind Zeromski's casket (in the "Funeral Rhapsody" in that writer's honor) and then "secretly mourn the poet at night," "orphaned and veiled in grief like a widow." (The "word" is often also personified in *The Salt of the Earth;* in fact there is a connection between language as a widow and the word "war" in the Prologue to that book—war which comes into the world with a "mournful train.") The poet's heart is personified like an "apache" in "The Elegy to the Eyes." There is an extended personification, embracing the whole poem, in "From the Song to the Music of the Future," in which gas, called ironically the "sweet siren's song" (another mythological allusion), addresses mankind, posing as a new Messiah. And often imagery in Wittlin's poems conforms to the theme of the poem. Thus in "Newspaper" we find "sheets of our pure souls" and "spoilage," as well as "printing" and "circulation." Wittlin likes to extend his images and make them all-embracing. In the "Lullaby to My Baby Daughter" (cf. the Appendix), we find in the same stanza: first, a comparison of sounds to shells; then of the baby's cradle to a "fortress" (rampart); and finally "an armor of nescience." In the preceding stanza sunrise is pictured as a victory of the dawn over the "troops of darkness."[6]

II *World War II*

However, Wittlin's poetic skill at first seemed to have forsaken him when the great disaster he so much dreaded and had so accurately predicted arrived and another Great War broke out

in 1939. Struck by horror he suddenly realized—as he confided
in an interesting talk "On the Communicability of the Arts,"
delivered at the Polish Institute of Arts and Science in New
York, November 26, 1967—that the traditional language of Polish
poetry was inadequate to this terrible reality. Nevertheless, in
1942 he composed a few poems of poignant beauty and the utmost simplicity, of that "secondary simplicity," which is achieved
only through great deliberation and a complete mastery over all
expressive means. They have been highly acclaimed by such
prominent Polish scholars and critics as the late Manfred Kridl
and Zbigniew Folejewski, and have appeared in every anthology
of the newer Polish verse. No translation, however successful,
can do justice to the nine rhymed couplets in which the story of
a Polish crucifixion is depicted in terms of the one universal
symbol of Holy and Sorrowing Motherhood. The poem's title is
the familiar Latin *Stabat Mater*[7] but already the first line translates the title into everyday Polish and adds the words "in the
market place." Here we have a Polish crucifixion which takes
place in the usual locale of execution in German-occupied Poland.
The Mother of God assumes the guise of a Polish mother in
poor maidservant's clothes ("w sluzacowskiej chustce")—who
does not even cry, but looks "with cold eyes at the cold dead
body" of her hanging son. The Polish coloring of this universal
scene of the greatest crime and the deepest suffering and sorrow
is enhanced by a naturalistic—unfortunately all too historical—
detail about the boots which had been taken away from the victim by the Germans. The detail serves as a natural transition to
another archetypal image—that of Mother-Earth—who suffers
and is silent, like the mother of the crucified son. In the second
part of this short poem, the first line (and the title) Stabat Mater
is repeated again, now in Latin, in order to link finally the Polish
event with the universal one. The next line is again in plain
Polish, forming a sharp and esthetically satisfying contrast to
the splendid eternal language of the Roman Catholic Church.
Finally, the Polish Mother, the Mother of God and Mother-Earth
are linked together in the image of Mother-Poland (Poland is
feminine in Polish)—*Mater nostra Polonia* (again in Latin), who
is crowned with the crown of thorns:

> Stabat Mater, Mater Nostra Polonia,
> A crown of thorns on her brow.

Thus a triple poetic expression of Holy and suffering Motherhood is merged into one symbol such as no Polish reader would bear to see ever again dissolved.

In the poem "To the Jews in Poland," also written in 1942, Wittlin admits that he has "no words" to express his overwhelming grief and pain at their fate and that his song bears the burden of their martyrs' blood with great difficulty. He asks: "Where are you, heavenly manna, in the new desert of the world?"[8] only to reply in his last stanza: "You are waiting for a miracle in vain, death wraps you up in paper." Almost a quarter of a century earlier, as a young man, he was still able to "cross the seas of blood" with "a new harvest of song" and hope, with a promise of manna falling, sweetening the bitter life (cf. "Prelude"). Then there was no more hope. His worst expectations and prophecies have materialized, exaggerated terribly and unbelievably by reality itself. Soon there was neither shrieking nor whispering to be heard but only the dead silence of sleepless nights for one, who was fulfilling the old tradition of a poet also a prophet suffering on behalf of many, indeed for all men, but suffering this time in silence. It is no accident that one of the most beautiful of Wittlin's poems, written in 1943, is addressed to "the Polish Language" and is not an ode, but a humble request to dispense "the last sacraments" to him and to all the others who are in exile with only the Polish language left to sustain them. Only their language can nourish spiritually the Polish soldiers and prisoners in their hour of trial, and can bid them farewell at their deaths. Characteristically, the poem ends with the following lines:

> And when we return to the gory bosom,
> Where you and we had our nascence—
> In Polish silence may angels greet
> The martyred land.
> *(Translated by Dorothy Meller; see Appendix)*

Thus like Norwid and Tuwim, like the nineteenth century Russian poet Fet (Shenshin) and like many another mystic, he resorts to silence as the deepest expression of one's emotions.

Whispers and silence are in fact Wittlin's forte. He even has been
called "a writer of the lowest tones," in reference to a book of his
essays.[9]

III   *New Poems of the 1960's*

Wittlin has continued to exercise his poetic vocation since
World War II. Along with some of his hymns, the Poets' and
Painters' Press in London brought out in February, 1969 six new
poems written in the 1960's. While these do not contribute anything essentially new to our image of Wittlin as a poet, they
prove that his lyre is still capable of more than one tone. Two
of the six are more in the nature of talks written in the form of
free verse poems (*gaweda* in Polish) on Biblical and ethical
topics. "The Lament of a Sacrificial Ram" (cf. Appendix for
Adam Gillon's translation of the poem) is somewhat reminiscent
of the "Pain of the Tree" ("trees do have a soul!"). It is delivered
by the ram which Abraham offered to God after the demand to
sacrifice Isaac had been dropped. The theme of Abraham's
offering (we may recall that Wittlin figures in the *Hymns* as a
"new Abraham") has fascinated Wittlin for a long time, as it
fascinated Kierkegaard before him, who remarked that if everything lies in the realm of the ethical, then Abraham is done for.
Wittlin, an avid reader of Kierkegaard, exclaimed in a book review, "Two war novels" (Dwie powiesci wojenne):[10] "Whose
death does not count?"—a rejoinder which could be applied just
as well to the insignificant unheroic hero of *The Salt of the Earth*
or to the hero of the "Hymn to a Spoonful of Soup" and of some
other hymns from which his "Saga of a Patient Foot Soldier" may
have evolved. With Wittlin every death counts, be it that of the
humblest of human beings, of an animal or a tree: they all have
a soul; the soul for Wittlin being an organ to experience pain.[11]
The dead bodies of animals are even more terrible to look at because they are more innocent.[12]

"The Lament of a Sacrificial Ram" vibrates with irony: the
leitmotif "because I do not have a soul" is repeated by the sacrificial ram five times with variations which prove the opposite,
of course! There is a dramatic quality to the "talk," the high
point of tension being the ram's switch to an invective: "And you
(Humans who have a soul, Z.Y.) what have you made of your
soul? A poisoned cistern in which your sundry crimes are nur-

tured. If only this: that your innocent must always suffer, perish for the guilty ones":

> Whole nations of two-legged scapegoats
> endowed with souls burn in crematoria,
> foul fumes beat against the vaults of heavens
> and yet no angels fly downward
> to stay the hangman's hands from murder.
> *(Translated by Adam Gillon)*

Thus, as is often the case with Wittlin, not only did an old cliché "scapegoat" receive a new expressive value, but it served as a frame for an entire poem which has acquired afresh a universal momentum. However, one must speak in this case of a certain verbosity which can also be found in some of his early works, notably in the *Hymns*. Wittlin has a predilection for bringing out "sharp points": "And only once in the earth's annals the animals were called brothers—by a holy man." Thus old motifs are again revived in his new poetry: we are back at the veneration of St. Francis of Assisi, a favorite theme with Wittlin.

The other "talk," entitled "From the Tree of Knowledge," tells the story of the destruction by an Italian farmer of a snake which hid in a tree in order to strangle birds. A parallel with the snake which had a human face and was really a devil is made at the very beginning of the "talk." Led by instinct the turkeys alarmed the Italian farmer Peppe who came and killed the snake. (The story takes place in "godly Monteluco" and is, as Wittlin has confided, a "real story.") Why—asks Wittlin—was there no Peppe in the Garden of Eden? With tongue-in-cheek he adds: "there probably were turkeys there too." Wittlin asks parenthetically: "But how could he have found himself in Paradise, if You had condemned to eternal sinless childlessness the parents of the human race. . . . And thus the cherubs and the fiery sword, the police. . . ." Wittlin has often told how he was struck as a child by the pictures of Adam and Eve being turned out of Paradise by a fiery angel with a sword. These early impressions have persisted throughout his life and found their way into a late poem, which tells us still more about Wittlin as man and poet. This last image in the poem may also serve as an explanation for the short apocalyptic piece which is included in the selection from

Poets' and Painters' Press of February, 1969. It is given here in its entirety:

Before the End of the World

Before the end of the world
Three angels appeared
on motorcycles.
One angel was dressed as a policeman:
He had a helmet on his head.
The other angel
wore a top hat and tuxedo.
The third angel . . .
wasn't an angel at all—
although he had winged arms
and a great radiance above his brow.

(Translated by Adam Gillon)

The poem is condensed, seemingly simple; its strength lies in the mixture of the metaphysical with the homely. Here an apocalyptic vision is clad in images so simple, in words so unassuming that they strike us as being almost inadequate. But it is not for nothing that Wittlin has defended homely and unimportant words as poetic: The vision of a supernatural visitation is created in a modern setting; an old motif, known to us from the first "Lullaby" in the *Hymns* is again revived. Characteristically, the last angel, the one with a halo around his head, is not an angel at all but, like the snake with a human head in the "From the Tree of Knowledge," a devil in disguise, a trick and substitution known to all mystics.

Wittlin's sharp satirical and saracastic edge protrudes in the poem called "Strictly Personal" and is aimed not at the lying and deceitful world—as all true Christians and poets know it to be—but at himself. The Biblical image of a human being created in God's image is at the root of the poem:

What does it want of me, this bald pate
which I must behold each time I shave?
I wish I could glimpse my soul in the mirror—just once
for I draw from it the tart essence of these words.

> You, who have created us in your own image
> and likeness, for a purpose known only to You,
> look upon me now: could You, Creator Divine,
> have a countenance as dreadful as mine?

And finally:

> While still alive, I smell my corpse's putrid odor;
> How, then, shall I not yearn for fragrant Paradise?
> But these false teeth chatter in fear—
> Shall I chew with them my Mother-Earth?
> *(Translated by Dorothy Meller)*

In addition to "Strictly Personal" he has a Biblical parable on the theme of Judas; the equation being Judas—false friends, who are "as stuffed with falsity as gefillte fish . . ."—which is called simply "Personal." The author recalls how he accidentally touched with his hand a hornets' nest and how his biting pain was assuaged by "milk and honey—the hope of the Promised Land"—only to conclude that the hornets' sting burnt him less than have the kisses of his Judas-friends.

These verses are both new and not new for Wittlin. The real intellectual tension, the emotional and intellectual charge so often previously present is here absent. However, Wittlin here gives a new treatment to age-old themes and motifs—no small achievement for anyone and a demonstration that age has not diminished his flexibility and growth. Formally the new poems are like the *Hymns*—free verse with only an occasional rhyme to stress some point.

IV   *Versification and Rhyme*

In Wittlin's poetry, as in Polish modern poetry in general, there is a peaceful coexistence of syllabic, accentual and accentual-syllabic prosodies of traditional and free verse, as well as of exact and inexact rhymes, that is assonance. In the few samples of his poetry written in traditional meters and also in those where accents count more than syllables—he shows himself to be a brilliant versifier.[13] In addition to metrical inventiveness, he also knows how to achieve variations in stanzaic form: he has traditional quatrains and stanzas of 5, 6, 8, 11 and 12 lines. He is

drawn to free verse which he infuses with ever new rhythms. And
when he does resort to rhymes, he uses a great variety of them:
exact and inexact rhymes, omonymic ones, rhymes created with
the help of foreign words or names which have the effect of an
unexpected sonority. He also likes internal rhymes which grace
his parallelisms and sometimes his antitheses. Whole poems are
built upon parallelisms; for instance, "Christmas-Eve Song on
Adam Mickiewicz" (where Adam Mickiewicz, who was born on
Christmas Eve is compared to Jesus Christ) or juxtapositions e.g.,
"Penitence in Assisi," (where well-to-do modern travelers to Assisi
are brought into sharp contrast with the figure of the Poverello).
Refrains and leitmotifs are used very effectively, helping him to
achieve a unity in composition and "variations on the theme."
The later poems are rich in overt and hidden sonorities; he always
tries to create musical effects, always regrets that he has not become a composer. However, in order to evaluate the melodiousness and musicality of his verse one must know it in the original.

The critics have raised the same objection: Why did he write
so little poetry? An original, aloof figure, he has always been
praised even when the schools with which he was connected
more or less loosely were sharply criticized. Czeslaw Milosz
singles him out from among all the Polish Expressionists of the
Poznan group as the one powerful poetic individuality. When
Jan Stur praised the *Hymns* and called Wittlin "our greatest
hope" he was certainly right in his early judgment; his words in
the same article[14] sum up Wittlin's whole output as poet, novelist,
essayist and translator. He called Wittlin an adherent to "ethical
responsibility" in the deepest essence of life: in experience and
its expression; not by the scales of gold but on the scales of his
conscience does he weigh every word.

Perhaps it is this factor, besides his metaphysical and philosophical (mostly existential), tinge that has so endeared him to
the poets of the new generation, to the postwar generation of
philosophical poets who avoid the "empty" words so hateful to
Wittlin, and who are seeking new depths in the riches of the
Polish tongue, capable of so many metamorphoses and mutations.

CHAPTER 3

Wittlin's Odyssey: *Three Versions*

T HREE versions have appeared of Joseph Wittlin's translation of the *Odyssey* from the original Greek into Polish
verse. The first, which appeared in 1924, was even then hailed
as an important event in the history of Polish literature; the
second appeared in 1931 when he was thirty-five and was awarded
a prize by the Polish P.E.N. Club; the third version appeared
only in 1957.

Wittlin began his translation of the *Odyssey* while he was still
a high-school student attending a classical Gymnasium in Lwów,
but it was World War I that actually engendered this new Polish
Odyssey. Alexander the Great used to carry the *Odyssey* with him
on his campaigns, the French writer Paul Cazin took his *Odyssey*
with him to the front, and Wittlin experienced such a spiritual
rebirth in the process of rediscovering the old familiar classic
that he continued to work at his translation even in a military
hospital.[1]

Wittlin's vision of Homer at that time was deeply influenced
by the brilliant Polish poet, dramatist and painter, Stanislaw
Wyspianski (1869-1907), a great genius of the Polish Symbolist
movement ("Young Poland"). Wyspianski, a forerunner of the
modern theatre, was largely responsible for the Homeric Renaissance (to use George de F. Lord's expression) in Poland at the
turn of the century. His dramatic trilogy, *Achilleis, Akropolis,*
and especially the *Return of Odysseus (Powrot Odyssa)*[2]—the last
not completed because of his untimely death, exerted a powerful
influence on the imagination of poets and readers of the younger
generation. An added factor was the language of the famous
Polish novelist Stefan Zeromski (1864-1925), another powerful
representative of "Young Poland," who advocated using archaic
language and used it himself, especially in such epic works as

Duma o Hetmanie (A Ballad on the Hetman),[3] which impressed the young Wittlin. Two great figures, Richard Wagner and Friedrich Nietzsche, must be regarded as at least partially responsible for the tragic atmosphere which pervades Wittlin's brilliant essay on Homer and on the art and craft of poetic translation. It appeared as a preface to his 1924 version and was reprinted in 1931. Its keynote is the idea: "Homer's Fatherland is Pain," which sounds surprisingly modern if we compare it with the words of the distinguished Homeric scholar, George E. Dimock, Jr., who says, "There is no human identity in other terms than pain."[4]

I Greek Myths in Polish Peasant Costume

It was most probably Wyspianski's clothing of the old Greek myths in Polish peasant costume (a technique fashionable with the Polish Symbolists at that time) that led Wittlin to make his first version, *Odyssey I*[5] a little too rustic and "peasanty" and perhaps also led him to overstress archaisms. But archaizing can also serve as a way of renovating poetic language and diction, which had become rather shopworn at the beginning of the twentieth century.[6]

Like the Romantics before them, the Polish Symbolists (often called Neo-Romantics) advocated the use of a special poetic language, the "language of poets and gods" (in the phrase of Baratynsky, a Russian Romantic). The object of this special language was to remove the reader from everyday reality and transport him onto a different plane of existence. Such a language gravitates naturally towards archaisms and dialect words and turns of phrase. The latter were also in tune with the trend toward rusticity and a peasant-flavored style. Wittlin used archaisms and quasi-dialect forms, and even coined many new words and derivatives[7] to freshen and defamiliarize the poetic language of his translation, to enhance its emotional expressiveness and effectiveness.

II Problems in Rendering Greek Hexameters

As in English, there are problems in rendering Greek hexameters into Polish. Previous translators of Homer had used either a traditional Polish 13-syllable line[8] or a Polish equivalent for the Homeric hexameter—a 16-syllable line with a definite caesura, mostly 8+8 syllables—rather unsuccessfully.[9] Wittlin was the first poet of stature who succeeded in preserving the poetic values of Homer's epic without sacrificing fidelity to the original. In Wittlin's hands—unlike those of his predecessors—a hexameter is a flexible medium, highly adaptable to different moods. It is sensitive to the tone of the story and can vary with the particular situation; it can show the acceleration of movement, the explosion of passion, the diminution of strength and its passing into fatigue.[10] For Wittlin, rhythm is quite rightly for the ear, and he cites Book XXII in his Preface with its rhythmic and arhythmic patterns expressing the tense atmosphere surrounding the murders or the beginning of Book XXIV with its funeral-march tempo, to illustrate his point.[11] He tried to be true to the changing rhythms of Homer with their multiple variations and to give the Polish reader a comparable experience in his native tongue.

"If the translation is not a poem, it fails to imitate the most important aspect of the original," writes George de F. Lord in his highly interesting and readable book on Chapman's Homer.[12] Wittlin calls all prose translations of Homer's *Odyssey* "super-prosaic"—no matter how faithful they are to the original—and he believes that instead of bringing the reader closer to Homer they only push him further away.[13] His aim as a translator of Homer and cocreator of the Polish *Odyssey* was to affect his readers' sensitivity and make them reflect on the actual values of the work rather than merely acquainting him with the story of Odysseus' trials and tribulations, which were after all well-known to Wittlin's contemporaries, most of whom had received a Classical education at school. He expected to achieve this by his rendition of the *melos* of the Homeric epic. According to Wittlin—and it is difficult not to agree with him—it is precisely the *song* that creates the form, the *Gestalt*, of the narrated event, bringing out its contours and shedding new lights upon them. While a prose translation of Homer's masterpiece can only inform us of the fate of the protagonists, the form of the poem in our own tongue enables us to feel the metaphysical qualities of Homer's work and gives us a poetic interpretation of the fate of its heroes.[14]

And it is of course precisely the metaphysical qualities of Homer's epic that have always most attracted Wittlin. In the early 1920's, while he was still working on the first version of his translation, he came to believe that Homer and his epic had a special relevance for his generation, the first "lost" postwar generation of modern times. For Wittlin, Odysseus and his wanderings came to symbolize the human soul and its wanderings in its eternal search for itself. How important this idea has become for him is shown by the fact that he, who is normally so critical of his own youthful writings, repeated it thirty years later in the Preface to *Odyssey III:* "Who are we people of the twentieth century, and where is the fatherland of our soul?"[15] In 1957 he repeated with even stronger conviction than before that human beings were "wanderers upon the immense ocean of life . . . longing for our primordial Fatherland which lies beyond the sea, yonder where we hope to find a nest of happiness."[16] However, he added a pessimistic note to this youthful cry: "Now we know that this primordial Fatherland, this mystical land flowing with milk and honey, this Ithaca, cannot be found beyond any sea, any river, any mountain—for it does not exist on this earth."[17]

III *Wittlin's and Gogol's Utopia*

Wittlin's 1924 Preface clearly showed that while presenting his contemporaries with a new Polish *Odyssey*—a labor of love into which he had put so much of himself—the poet-translator hoped eagerly that the old classic might help to fill the void he sensed so keenly in their minds and hearts. He was attracted by the idea of a modern utopia and hoped to fascinate his readers with the intimacy between gods and men he had himself felt so strongly in Homer and the Bible. Could the *Odyssey* awaken in its modern readers the longing for a new communion between gods and men? Wittlin's hopes for his expressionistic utopia remind one that the great Russian writer Nikolai Gogol (1809-1852) hoped when his friend Vassily Zhukovsky (1783-1852) published a new translation of the *Odyssey,* that it would change the way of life of the Russian people, and bring about a new closeness between man and God.[18] And so one is tempted to suggest that the poetic conventions of the "Young Poland" movement were not the only barrier intervening between the Greek original and Wittlin's first two versions: there were also the translator's own personality and his youthful vision of utopia.

IV   *"Music" and "Metaphysics"*

The Polish Symbolists of the "Young Poland" School, as well as many other Symbolists and Expressionists, believed in a mysterious connection between the "metaphysics" of a literary work and its "music." In accordance with this belief, Wittlin sought to impress Homer's images and ideas upon the imagination of his readers by extensive repetitions, an elaborate interplay of sounds and frequent alliterations of various kinds. He built up and swelled the upsurge of rising emotions with numerous interjections, exclamations and pauses. He added color to words by attaching to them diminutive, emotion-laden suffixes. In *Odyssey III*, however, all these devices are almost completely abandoned. The repetitions are drastically reduced, sometimes from three or four down to a single one, or even eliminated entirely. For instance, at the end of Book XXIII, speaking about Calypso *Odyssey I* and *II* have: "She will be unable; oh, she will not be able to persuade his faithful heart . . .!" *Odyssey III* has merely: . . . "but in vain: she did not manage to captivate his faithful heart," thus eliminating from only one sentence an interjection, a repetition, a pause, and an exclamation mark. In the same Book we have an emotionally colored description of the song of the Sirens: "And how he listened to the wail of the Sirens' languorous song that captivates, lures, and enchants the soul with its charm (*Odyssey I* and *II*), which in *Odyssey III* becomes "And how he listened to the seductive song of the Sirens. . . ."

In *Odyssey I* and *II* there are many instances where an emotion is supported by interplay of sounds—alliteration, assonance, internal rhyme, and the like; but in *Odyssey III* many of these were eliminated or altered, initial alliteration in particular being avoided as foreign to the genius of the Polish language.

V   *Poetic Diction of the "Young Poland" Movement*

Poetic diction, as the "Young Poland" movement thought of it, must be conspicuous and unusual, not to say exotic. Accordingly, we find in *Odyssey I* overabundant emotional epithets (terrible, bitter, mournful and the like), the excessive use of personal pronouns which have a great expressive charge, a fondness for "precious" superlatives (most terrible, most patiently, etc.), archaic and dialect forms which frequently supply more melodious variants. However, fashions change, and so did Wittlin's taste. Words and features that were then much in fashion (and which were later used to parody the "Young Poland" style) are very frequent in *Odyssey I*, less so in *Odyssey II*, while in *Odyssey III* they have practically disappeared. Folk and peasant elements were particularly prominent in *Odyssey I*, but tended to be changed or replaced in the subsequent versions. Thus "homestead" in *Odyssey I* becomes "palace" in *Odyssey II*, and simply "rooms" in *Odyssey III*. The "wench" Artemis of *Odyssey I* is changed into the "immaculate" Artemis in *Odyssey III*, Zeus's "wenches" of *Odyssey I* also disappear in *Odyssey III*. At the beginning of Book XXIV, Achilles no longer holds the reins in his hands—holding the reins was now seen as much too "peasantlike" an activity. Wittlin sidesteps the issue in *Odyssey III*.

VI   *Three versions of* Odyssey *further compared*

If we compare *Odyssey I* and *Odyssey II*, we find the main differences to be the removal of the rustic elements, some pruning of the "Young Poland" "poetic diction," the elimination of some paired synonyms (e.g., "roar and groan," etc.), the excision of excessive periphrasis and metonymy and some restraints on the archaizing tendency.

However, if we compare all three versions we find that Wittlin has remained essentially faithful to the principle of archaizing in rendering the ancient Greek classic. While he does avoid some Church Slavicisms and some Old Polish morphological and syntactic features that he had freely used in the two earlier versions, *Odyssey III* still contains a large number of archaizing expressions. He has been especially reluctant to part with words that helped him to achieve the harmony of sound that was so important to him. Sometimes he even retained in all versions a word that he had publicly "renounced";[19] e.g., Old Polish *spyza*, "food," or specially created for the sake of its sound, and sometimes, contrary to the rules of Old Polish grammar,[20] he kept such otherwise unknown expressions as *ocemgnieniu* or *oczymgnieniu* (in the twinkling of an eye) based on the Old Polish dual, a special grammatical form for paired objects like eyes or feet. Wittlin's own coinages—more and less felicitous—are to be found in all three versions, imparting to them a generally archaic atmosphere.

He is particularly fond of such suffixes as -acz, -arz, and -nik (the last a suffix that in recent years has been very productive in English as well!).

Indeed, a detailed and thorough comparison of the three versions of Wittlin's *Odyssey* would make a fascinating study of changing taste and style in modern Polish poetry. Even without using computers and statistics—possibly desirable tools in this case—it is clear that the third version strives toward more concrete expression and more vivid imagery. Older "poetic" expressions that have lost their connotative and evocative power are replaced, and the changes show Wittlin's inventiveness, his increasing mastery of the craft of poetry, his unerring sense of the language. The three successive *Odysseys* reflect all the major changes in Polish style of the period as it gradually began to free itself from its excessive overgrowth of imagery and "poetic" expression.

As we progress through the *Odysseys*, we find vague "poetical" or periphrastic expressions giving way to more concrete, matter-of-fact, and sometimes even technical words. Thus a "young cow that has not calved" becomes simply a "heifer," "skins eaten away by decay" (which has some Expressionistic overtones) becomes "skins dried and mouldered away," the quiver "abounding with shafts and whistling arrows" at the beginning of Book XXII becomes more vividly and concretely "chock-full of swiftly-flying arrows." Some poetic sounding birds (turtle-dove, sparrow-hawk) disappear from the text, as does an exotic flower, the lotus (for which the Polish Symbolists had shown a great liking), to be replaced, prosaically but more accurately by "wheat, barley, and clover." The new words are not necessarily more prosaic; e.g., the nondescript "plains" of *Odyssey II* become "the steppe" which is more evocative for a Polish reader. *Odyssey I* and *Odyssey II* had fanciful names for the herbs which Helen puts into the drinks of Menelaus and Telemachus in Book IV—Sorrow-free, Wrath-free, Oblivion-of-all Evil. In *Odyssey III* these have disappeared.

Odyssey I and *II* have many examples of circumlocutory and nebulous writing with unnecessary periphrasis which are compressed and deflated in *Odyssey III;* e.g., "his forefathers' land" to "his fatherland"; "had his fireside" to "lived"; "far away from his fathers' soil" (peasant coloring) to "far from his own people."

An excess of diminutives, the overuse of periphrasis, exclamation points, pauses and interjections, all contributed to the strong emotional coloring of the two earlier versions which according to specialists is not in keeping with the Greek original. (E. V. Rieu remarks in his preface that one has to deliberate a long time before putting in an exclamation mark when translating Homer.)[21] In *Odyssey III* this emotional coloring is diluted, except in the speeches of gods and men under great emotional stress. Even in the vision of Theoclymenus, where in *Odyssey I* and *II* we find many pauses, as many as two in one line, or fourteen exclamation marks in nine lines, in *Odyssey III* we have only nine pauses and nine exclamation marks (generally combined thus: . . . !) in thirteen lines.

In *Odyssey III* Wittlin has worked out a much more refined way to express deep emotion, one that does not require excessive repetitions and exclamations. In Book XI, speaking of what Rieu calls "the City of Perpetual Mist,"[22] where the dead dwell, *Odyssey I* has an almost idyllic expression for "eternal night" (*nocka wieczysta*) with a diminutive suffix -*k*; *Odyssey II* has "night eternal" without the diminutive suffix; while *Odyssey III* has a highly evocative description in which "night eternal" and "death-giving night" are used side-by-side, forming a gradation and are reinforced by "mortals." A little later in the same book Wittlin uses the epithet "nightly," and here we can catch a glimpse of how he has achieved his closely-woven, dense poetic texture. This "nightly" is highly evocative because it reminds us of the "death-giving night": Odysseus, in Hades, meets the shade of Elpenor, who had fallen off the roof and been killed as they were leaving Circe's island. "O, Elpenor, how did you stumble into this *nightly* darkness?"

The epithet *czarowny* "charming," used in *Odyssey I*, was becoming rather trite in contemporary Polish, so it was replaced by "noble and magic" in *Odyssey III*. The "blessed" soil of Egypt that gives birth to various poisons in Book IV is changed to "fertile soil," sacrificing the witty oxymoron but gaining in concreteness and closeness to the original.

Generally speaking, Wittlin's epithets in *Odyssey III* parallel Homer's. He eliminated the peasant and poetic epithets he had introduced under Symbolist influence and came up with some splendid denotative ones to replace them: a "vaulted" wave, a "blown-out" wave. He showed great ingenuity in reproducing Homer's famous compound epithets, which have created such grave problems for so many translators of Homer e.g., "bitter-salty wastes" (*gorzko-slone pustacie*), "sharp-eyed," "eternal and eternally young." Homer's recurrent epithets sometimes become unbearable to a modern reader. When this happens, Wittlin varies the epithet. Odysseus is called not only "wise" and "very wise" but also "resourceful," "versatile," "experienced," "most experienced" as well as "trickster," "crafty," "shifty," etc., depending on who is speaking about him; one of his friends, an enemy, or Homer himself.

In *Odyssey III*, dialect and archaizing features are removed entirely when Homer himself is the narrator, but are preserved when the heroes are talking, as for example where Odysseus is the narrator (Books IX-XII), Wittlin freely uses archaic and dialect forms that he excludes from Homer's own speech. Books IX-XII are peppered by Wittlin with archaic and dialect forms and slangy expressions, making it evocative and expressive, and thereby creating "a narrative manner which focuses on the personal 'tone' of the fictional narrator."[23] This technique called *skaz* by Russian Formalists, invests the archetypal versatile hero with yet another dimension.

The emotional tone of Circe's speech to Odysseus at the end of Book X, or of Elpenor's plea in Book XI, and its impact on the reader are heightened by the use of archaic expressions, repetitions, and even rhymes (which are generally absent elsewhere in Wittlin's translation as they are absent in Homer).

While authors and critics have long been concerned and will for the foreseeable future continue to be concerned with the question of what degree of archaizing is desirable for the translations when Homer himself is speaking, a much more difficult question is to decide on the individual coloring to be given to the speeches of the various characters by the translator. In his early preface, Wittlin quips that Homer in Hades gives personal interviews to interested scholars on all such 64-dollar questions. Characters like Circe, the Cyclops, the shade of Elpenor, are given strong emotional coloring by an expressive mixture of archaisms and dialectisms. For instance, the Cyclops, after being blinded, addresses his favorite ram, *tryku* (a dialect word), *serdenko* (diminutive suffix with emotional coloring, a regional word).

Between 1924 and 1957 Wittlin also learned better how to capture the flavor of aggressive speech, even to its ironic overtones. If we compare the three versions of the argument between Odysseus and Irus in Book XVIII we note a marked successive improvement in individualization and lifelike expressiveness through the use of racy colloquialisms and slang. In this passage "the lust of my hungry intestines" *(Odyssey I)* becomes more and more colloquial and vivid, first "my ignoble stomach" *(Odyssey II)* and finally "my scamp of a stomach" *(Odyssey III)*.

All these nuances helped Wittlin to revitalize still more his *Odyssey* and, according to specialists, to do better justice to Homer's primordial freshness and simplicity which shuns everything conspicuous and unusual. It was Wittlin's talent for refreshing and revitalizing shopworn words and images, discarding everything that had lost its evocative power, that saved him from many pitfalls even in the early stages of his translation of the *Odyssey*. He was justified in saying he had served his apprenticeship in the school of Homer.[24]

We cannot easily assess the degree to which Wittlin by his *Odyssey* has succeeded in bringing about a new intimacy between gods and men. We know, however, that through translating the great Greek classic he mastered the difficult idiom of religious and mythical beliefs so well that he was even able to parody that idiom in his later novel, *The Salt of the Earth* (cf. Chapter V). It was his work on this translation which helped to sharpen his pen still more and made his vision even more observant. From Homer he was learning economy and the art of condensation, which he was later able to put to good use in his original work.[25]

This comparison of the various versions of Wittlin's translation, while not pretending to anything approaching completeness, nevertheless permits us to draw certain conclusions about the general growth of his art as a poet and about his creative maturity. Prone to parody and irony, and gifted with a fine nose to ferret out anything eclectic, stilted or worn-out in current poetic styles, he kept on revising his translation so as to avoid offending his own sensibilities, which were not infrequently more advanced than those of his contemporaries.

VII   Odyssey II *and* Odyssey III *during World War II*

Many more examples could be introduced to show how thoroughly Wittlin reworked his 1931 version of the *Odyssey* during the Second World War. Homer, who had proved such a worthy companion and friend during the First World War, again occupied his mind during the Second. In his Preface to *Odyssey III* he explained that in 1944, the year of the battle of Monte Cassino and the Insurrection of Warsaw, he was thinking of "our new Odysseuses and Telemachuses" who needed a more balanced and austere presentation and a simpler diction as a counterweight to the earthshaking events and adventures they were being subjected to. But even so, he could never renounce the *melos*, the music and the poetry of the Greek, in order to make his translation popular. And in the Second World War, Wittlin's version of the *Odyssey* proved to be as effective and salutary for young people in distress as his work on the first version had been for him alone during World War I. A young Polish poet, Tadeusz Gaycy (1922-44) who perished in the Warsaw Insurrection, wrote a play called *Homer and the Orchid*, markedly influenced by Wittlin's *Odyssey II*, especially in its exuberant, buoyant rhythms. This play about Homer's blindness was produced, secretly of course, in German-occupied Warsaw. Another Polish poet, Boleslaw Micinski (1911-43), also composed a drama in the style of Wittlin's *Odyssey*. Wittlin ascribed his *Odyssey III* to the memory of these two poets.[26]

VIII   *The Polish* Odyssey

Only time will tell which translation will become the true Polish *Odyssey*. When Lucjan Siemienski's verse translation of Homer's classic appeared in 1873 it was acclaimed as such. However, Professor S. Srebrny, a great authority on classical antiquity, in his review of *Odyssey II* stressed numerous points on which it was superior to Siemienski's. Indeed he judged it to be better as a whole especially because it was so much closer to the mood and tone of the Greek original.[27]

When the third version of Wittlin's *Odyssey* appeared in London it was enthusiastically welcomed and highly acclaimed by the Polish critic Zygmunt Kubiak, known as a connoisseur of ancient literature, especially Greek. Kubiak's article bore the significant title: "The Polish Homer."[28]

Often the literary-historical "perspective," is clouded by extraneous considerations. In present day Poland Jan Parandowski's (b. 1895) very lucid prose translation of the *Odyssey* has become a best-seller and enjoys as great popularity as E. V. Rieu's in the English-speaking world. When Parandowski, who had been "godfather" of Wittlin's *Odyssey*[29] and had written an extremely favorable review of Wittlin's first version, *Odyssey I,* published excerpts of his own translation, he assailed all his predecessors in no uncertain terms. In another article which appeared in a symposium entitled *On Translation,* edited by Michal Rusinek, Parandowski once more dwelled upon the superiority of a prose translation of Homer over a poetic rendering. The English summary of the article contains a passage that shows that not only poetic translations, but even prose summaries in one language of articles in another, may contain gross inaccuracies: "The author thinks that the great popularity of his translation, which attained a greater number of editions than any other and found its way to readers who had hardly heard of Homer before, is the best proof that his method (i.e., prose translation) was right."[30]

Nothing of the sort, however, can be found in Parandowski's article, of which this purports to be an abstract for the English-speaking reader. Indeed one can hardly measure the value of a translation or its method by the number of copies it sells, especially in the present instance where all other relevant facts are so unequal: Parandowski is a noted writer in Poland, who enjoys great popularity there for many reasons; Wittlin is in exile, an émigré writer. His works, including the *Odyssey,* have not been admitted into Poland for a long time (even when sent as gifts to his numerous friends).

And in fact *Odyssey III* acquired new dimensions under Wittlin's pen, such as could only have come from a man fated for permanent exile. The eternal romance of human wanderings and sufferings, which can be read on so many levels, has been deepened and sharpened by the poet-translator's own experience, acquiring a new relevance for all those who are still homeless and longing to return to their native Ithaca. To quote one more perceptive appraisal of Wittlin's final version: Wittlin has been transformed into the "cocreator of the epic" because "the motif of wandering, of longing, of homecoming, has become one of the predominant features of his inspiration."[31]

Even as far back as 1924, Wittlin admitted that he had put so much of himself into his *Odyssey* that he could no longer regard it as just a translation. How much more must this feeling have deepened after so many years of intimate association with his beloved bard and "eternal companion"—to use Merezhkovsky's expression. There are indeed many links between the *Odyssey* and Wittlin's original work, as has been pointed out.

It is still too early to pass final judgment on the merits of Wittlin's or Parandowski's translation. But it was Wittlin's poetic Polish *Odyssey* that has been called a "classic stylization" which enchants with its "lightness and simplicity," two innate features of any truly classical art.[32] Moreover, this translation is the work of one of the finest Polish poets of modern times. Indeed, "translation" is an inadequate term to describe Wittlin's *Odyssey*. Rather we might speak of a "communion of saints"—a phrase Wittlin himself uses to describe Boris Pasternak's "communion" with Shakespeare.

CHAPTER 4

The Salt of The Earth:
Exposing the War Myth

> Art is always and incessantly pre-
> occupied with two things—it is con-
> stantly concerned with death, and
> constantly transforms it into life.
> Boris Pasternak

I *Exposing the War Myth*

WITTLIN, already thoroughly familiar with Greek, Babylonian and other myths, now set out to examine the myths
of the twentieth century as well as to create a few of his own.
In the years after the First World War, as is evident from his
Hymns and his postwar books and essays (e.g., *War, Peace and
The Soul of The Poet*) his mind was still absorbed by the war,
and in *The Salt of the Earth* he began to "settle his accounts
with it," to use a phrase he himself had used in connection with
Joseph Roth.[1]

He volunteered to serve in the Eastern Polish Legion, and
then in the Austro-Hungarian Army. Brought up on the "mystical"
food of Polish patriotic songs and deeds, he still believed—before
his actual experience with military life began—that killing in war,
especially in defense of the freedom of one's homeland, was very
different from killing in general. But his convictions changed
completely while he was in the army, particularly under the
influence of his enlightened, saintly friend, Ludwik Brudzinski,
who perished in the war. Brudzinski made Wittlin see that there
was only one kind of killing and that all killing was antihuman
and anti-Christian.

Wittlin's war experiences became the core of this book which
was designed to examine and to destroy the war myth, to laugh
it out of existence, by turning it into absurdity. One should not

exaggerate, however, the importance of the author's personal experience in opposition to his "achieved content," the term Max Schorer proposes for the artistic presentation—the "form," of a literary work.[2] It has become a truism to say that the "what" and the "how" merge in an esthetic object. "Every new content inevitably appears in art as form."[3] For Wittlin—the poet and translator of Homer in verse—prose was a new form.[4] Before he began to write his "saga of the patient foot soldier" (the subtitle of *The Salt of the Earth*), he had "composed" a "Requiem For Those Who Fell In the World War" (*Requiem za poleglych na wojnie*) designed to be recited by "soloists" and choruses.[5] He had also started work on the poem on the theme of the Unknown Soldier. We can also agree with the critic Ludwik Fryde, that the saga of the patient foot soldier grew out of his "Hymn to a Spoonful of Soup."[6] The complicated problem of the distinction between poetry and prose, especially as regards rhythm, could be illuminated, if not solved, by detailed comparisons of the "Hymn," "The Requiem," and *The Salt of the Earth*. In Wittlin's highly poetic and "musical" prose one can even find some recurring rhythmical units of a kind usually associated with verse.

II *The Genre of* The Salt of the Earth

The genre of *The Salt of the Earth* presents a similarly complex question. When the book finally appeared in 1935 (it had been ten years in the making!), it evoked varied critical appraisals. It was described as a novel, but also as "not a novel in the strict sense,"[7] "a tale of a lyric poet,"[8] "a factual (terse) novel,"[9] "a classical epic,"[10] "a poem,"[11] to cite only the most important opinions. Wittlin himself called the whole cycle (the work was planned in three parts) a *roman fleuve* before its publication,[12] and then a "cryptopoem" after its appearance in print.[13] One is almost inclined to agree with Northrop Frye's sweeping observation that "most critical efforts to handle such generic terms as 'epic' and 'novel' are chiefly interesting as examples of the psychology of rumor."[14] That matters have not changed or improved in the past third of a century, can be seen from more recent evaluations of the book, which have defined it as a "sociological novel,"[15] a book written "in the grand style of European naturalism,"[16] and a book in which Polish customs of the early twentieth century can be studied.[17] How is one to choose from this medley of opinions? One can respond, of course, that a novel is a Protean genre, that, on the one hand, the word "novel" is widely misused, and that, on the other hand, the epic in the twentieth century is different from the epic of previous centuries. However, it may be possible to resolve the apparent contradiction in terms of Wittlin's own distinction of the novel as a *"roman fleuve"* and a "cryptopoem." In his article on the modern French "epic" Wittlin clarifies the problem to some extent: "We must say in all honesty that for some time now every worthwhile novel with a deep insight into historical details and an impartial portrayal of the spiritual processes forced by the pressures of overriding necessity has been an epic poem."[18]

In the same article he calls Flaubert's *Madame Bovary* "an example of a great psychological, epic poem," referring to works by Hamsun and Conrad as epic poems in which the authors "have succeeded in preserving to the very end their almost superhuman incognito. . . ."[19] These pronouncements shed some light upon the problem of the genre of *The Salt of the Earth* which can be regarded from one standpoint as a novel, though not in the strictest sense of the word, but which can also be elevated to the status of an epic, an epic "with a difference"—i.e., an epic of the twentieth century. One could also apply to it the term "poem," although again not at all in an unequivocal sense.[20] One could cite several other articles[21] in which Wittlin has expressed concern over the contemporary decline of the art of the epic, and has voiced hopes for its possible revival. He proposed to breathe new life into this rapidly expiring genre. From an epic writer of our century, he demanded an absolutely objective manner bordering on indifference; although this objectivity might only be apparent, allowing the reader to discern the author's loves and hates behind the screen of impartiality. He expected the epic writer to be able to depict things great and small, important and seemingly unimportant, with equal mastery and evocative power. He wanted him to be able not only to reproduce creatively all the characteristic features of the milieu even in the most minute detail, but to be able to recreate its soul, "the soul of the movement, the soul of the noise, of the silence, of the battle."[22] We see here the expressionist attraction to the "soul," the spirit, harmonizing with Wittlin's own metaphysical longings, his efforts to discover the real substance of things.

While he pondered over the possibilities for a further development of the epic art, the prevailing taste in post-World War I Poland tended towards authenticity, a more realistic, and matter-of-fact approach in art, which would register facts, both historical and psychological. There is no denying that Wittlin himself experienced some of this "hunger for authenticity," to quote his own expression, and checked over every single detail of the material contained in his book. But neither can one deny that all these "realia" and details which he so painstakingly verified had for the most part only one aim: to win the reader's confidence by telling him of mythical events in a tone one normally reserves for real events. Wittlin's objective was to explore and "explode" the war myth of the twentieth century, and at the same time to create his own myths, although these "myths" are always closely related to the realities of history.

His poem on the theme of the Unknown Soldier gradually began to assume a different form. The rhythms of its stanzas receded, and the poem began to take on the semblance of a story which could be readily accepted by a reader geared to the genre of the novel. This "novel as a poem" can thus be read on many levels. The less perceptive reader would be satisfied with its purely narrative aspect, while the more perceptive will be able to perceive its ironic and metaphorical aspects as well.

Wittlin has often stated that one of his greatest teachers was Homer. We know what his own translations of the *Odyssey* have meant to him. It is natural, therefore, that the subject of war was for him indissolubly linked with Homer. Indeed, according to Wittlin, Homer was not primarily concerned with the depiction of battle, and he condemned war at the very beginning of the *Iliad*. To Wittlin, Homer was an epic writer who happened to have lived during a bloody period of history, and who sought to portray man's lot in the most intense moments of his times: at Troy, in the heat of battle. "Was Leo Tolstoy a battle painter for the sake of the battle?" Wittlin asked in an interview. Of course not, and yet he has created the most perfect war epic since the time of Homer.[23]

III   The Salt of the Earth *and Other War Books*

Comparisons have been drawn between *The Salt of the Earth* and *War and Peace*. Even at first glance, however, there are more observable differences between the two books than similarities. The most significant difference concerns the two writers' very dissimilar artistic techniques. Tolstoy is a meticulous collector of the details which make up life in all its rich variety; he thereby creates a vast complex artistic "field of vision." Wittlin, on the other hand, works as a poet: he synthesizes his material, crystallizing it into a few words which are sustained and accentuated by the rhythm of his language. This does not preclude a certain epic *rozlewnosc* (prolix style) nor a lyrical linking of material on the associative principle. Thus, to understand and to enjoy the depth of meaning and art of Wittlin's prose, we must read very attentively—just as attentively as we read poetry, without skipping a single work, to say nothing of skipping several pages at a time, as many a reader of Tolstoy has done![24]

The Salt of the Earth has also been compared with Remarque's well-known bestseller *All Quiet on the Western Front (Im Westen nichts Neues)*. Except for the similarity of theme in the two books, there is nothing to justify such a comparison.[25] Remarque depicts the conflicts between the recruits and their sergeants on a purely physical plane, listing the many fantastic assignments the sergeants think up to torment the enlisted men. Wittlin recreates a highly complex relationship between his "unknown soldier," Peter Niewiadomski, and his "unknown sergeant," Rudolph Bachmatiuk, a sergeant "with a difference," who would like to subjugate not only the soldier's body, but his soul as well. As civilian clothes are replaced by uniforms, thus discarding "the old Adam," (Bachmatiuk is able to recognize individual differences among human beings only after they have been clad in uniform!) so, too, the soul is replaced by the rifle, the most important part of the infantryman, a much more precious one to him than his heart or his brain! Shunning hackneyed themes, characters and literary devices as much as he has shunned stylistic clichés, Wittlin did not want to create merely another sergeant "chewing out" his subordinates. He captured the essence of this particular type; although Bachmatiuk worships the army, he remains a real human being, capable of suffering, fear and guilt.

The fact that Wittlin's unknown soldier is a humble Hucul, a porter at the station of Topory-Czernielica, located in a quiet backwater of the Austro-Hungarian Empire, a man who cannot read or even tell his right hand from his left, inevitably suggests a comparison with the hero of Jaroslav Hasek's famous *Good Soldier Schweik*. Both Schweik and Peter are weak-minded heroes, but Wittlin's protagonist is not a "Polish Schweik."[26] The device of using a hero whose mind is unspoiled by sophistication, to set straight certain basic human values that have become distorted and to defamiliarize the usual trite round of commonplace facts and events, thus investing them with new life and expression, is a time-honored device in world literature. Voltaire, Chateaubriand, and Tolstoy used it for ironical and satirical purposes. This same category includes the long-established tradition of the "fool" who is frequently a wiser man. Both Hasek and Wittlin sought to show the absurdity of war. *The Salt of the Earth* is quite different from Hasek's novel in both artistic intent and execution. It is a much finer work of art, the product of a first-class critical and creative intellect. It is not a novel as a history, nor a novel as satire (like Hasek's)—but a "novel as a poem," in which Wittlin condenses certain historical facts and historical and unhistorical myths into pure crystals of poetry. Indeed, comparisons with other books only serve to illustrate more clearly unique values of *The Salt of the Earth*.

IV *A Modernized Epic*

Wittlin's book is an attempt to modernize the epic; he has chosen a familiar theme—the conduct of men during a great upheaval, treating it in a new way. The traditional epic devices such as prologue and epilogue, the commencement *in medias res,* the intrusion of supernatural powers, the use of dreams and omens, wide-ranging "broad-view" pictures, the leisurely presentation of details, *"die Totalität der Objekte"* (in Hegel's phrase), extended metaphors and similes, stock epithets, are all present in *The Salt of the Earth,* but they usually serve a different function. At times the grand style demanded by every definition of the epic is here applied to some insignificant events, thereby creating a tension between manner and matter; or, sometimes

the language may be dignified and poetic, even shot through
with pathos, and then, all of a sudden, display a mocking intent.
In this respect Wittlin's style resembles that of the great nine-
teenth-century Russian writer Nikolai Gogol.[27]

Epic features "with a difference" are especially conspicuous
in the Prologue to *The Salt of the Earth,* where we can also hear
echoes of the unfinished poem about the Unknown Soldier and
where we feel the author's presence. The Prologue is conceived in
an epic manner, dwelling on recent historical events, but it ends
unexpectedly with a quite ordinary episode in which a signalman
saves the life of a poor Jewish milkman crossing the railroad
tracks with his cart, in front of an onrushing military train. Thus,
also, supernatural powers are often reduced to the level of the
military and administrative powers which controlled and directed
people's destinies during the war. The hero himself is quite
unheroic: the officer in charge of the military train, enraged at
being halted at the crossing, calls him a "dope" and threatens
to report him; he is called a "dope" also by his immediate boss,
the stationmaster of Topory-Czernielica.

As Fryde has noted,[28] Wittlin has made a conscious and masterly application of the epic style to his saga. For example, while
at times he is very specific about historical dates, elsewhere he
will say (cf. Chapter 2) "some day" in a sense equivalent to
"once upon a time," or will even use the tone of a storyteller
addressing a close circle of listeners: "In those days human
bodies were weighed and measured . . ." (p. 71). He even addresses, as it were, distant posterity, explaining to it with cutting
irony our strange habit of saluting military superiors. . . . Always
skirting the boundary between the real and the mock epic,
Wittlin achieves a great intensity of expression and poetic condensation.

The War Lords, called by Wittlin "manufacturers of corpses"
in one of the *Hymns,* are presented first. Of these the Emperor
Franz Josef, a half-mythical, half-comical figure, surrounded by
his aides, is the most important.[29] He signs the declaration of war
under pressure from his entourage who have convinced him that
his "dear peoples" are demanding satisfaction for the death
of Archduke Franz Ferdinand. Personally Franz Josef hated
Franz Ferdinand and was glad to have survived his heir apparent.
And yet it was Ferdinand who was dictating this turn of events

from beyond the grave. Here Wittlin weaves a double strand of irony, the climax of which is reached at the moment when the Emperor, after signing his fateful proclamation partly in ink and partly in blood (like a mock Faust), utters this oracular judgment: "If I am not mistaken . . . blood will flow"[30] (p. 186). Thus too ink and blood merge as in Wittlin's poem "Newspaper" (cf. Chapter 2). Elsewhere in the novel he calls ink "a poisonous liquid."

In a manner imperceptible to the untrained eye, Wittlin introduces a mythology of his own. He is at his best not where he tries to be a scholar and meticulous researcher in the style of Flaubert, who liked to check every detail against scientific treatises or archaeological findings, but rather where he gives free rein to his imagination and reconstructs not the historical but the "mythico-historical process." Thus, he describes the inclined cross on St. Stephen's crown which "threatened to fall upon the old man's head" (p. 185). Much later, in Chapter 7, we learn the meaning of this "inclined cross" in Peter's interpretation: it indicates that faith is declining since Franz Josef reigns not only over Catholics but also over Protestants (in Hungary).

The Prologue is important for our understanding of the whole work because it contains subtle allusions and ambiguities which become clearer as the book progresses, and Parts Three and Four of the Prologue are especially important in this connection. In Part Three, which is composed like a song with a distinct beginning and ending, Wittlin describes the moment when the word "war" is being set in type in a print shop. The hand of the typesetter trembles and he picks up a wrong letter. The absurdity of the war is stressed by the appearance of the senseless word that comes out into the world while the typesetter washes his hands in a gesture reminiscent of Pilate, emphasizing the wickedness of the war. The same motif of absurdity can be found in Chapter 2, where Peter Niewiadomski, who is told to put up the declaration of war on the wall, does it upside down, since he cannot read and there are no pictures to help him decide which is the right side up. The tragicomic disorientation of the world is vividly, if indirectly conveyed by this image. Wittlin describes how the news of war spread throughout Vienna and other cities: "The news sped from mouth to mouth. The mouths chewed it, tasted it, turned it over, crunched it, till at last a million lips at once spat the one word onto the pavement, like a bitter almond" (p. 20).

Part Four of the Prologue is an epic picture—again in the form of a highly rhythmical song, shot through with much repetition, alliteration and assonance. It describes armies made up of the different nations mobilized by their emperors. Although clad in different uniforms they all tend to merge into a faceless mass, into "numbers of heads." The motif of parting and farewell resounds throughout this section; parting not only from families and loved ones, but "parting from their own individualities," the hardest of all separations. Using biblical allusions as satirical weapons, which he often does throughout the book, Wittlin says that people were throwing away "the old Adam" and donning the new uniforms. The established order, the established morality and law will soon be exchanged for a new order, a new law and morality. The departure of the mobilized men is everywhere accompanied by the sound of weeping: the writer describes the tears at the railway terminals of Vienna, Budapest and Prague, the wailing in the station waiting rooms at Lwów and Cracow, the tears of "the stations of Belgrade and St. Petersburg, of Moscow and Warsaw." Metonymy and personification make this account of lamentation dramatic and expressive. The motif of departure and death will be developed later, in Chapter 6, with lamentations framing the chapter and raising its tone to a truly epic level. The migration of peoples eastward and southward, from East to West, encompasses not only the land but the sea and air as well; and everywhere the weapons are ready for their destructive work. "Glory to Man in the heights, and on land, and under the water!" exclaims Wittlin mockingly. The battalions of the multilingual Empire cheer each other and bid each other farewell in different tongues. Later on, in Chapter 7, the "Tower of Babel" motif of the lack of communication among men who are to fight for a common cause will be developed in greater detail. To heighten the effect Wittlin gives the cheers of various nationalities in the Empire in several languages. *"Zivio! Hoch! Niech zyje! Hurrah! Evviva! Daj Boze hazard!"* Immediately after these high-spirited cries he creates an effect of sharp contrast by shifting to the completely different, more objective, if ironic, tone of a narrator: "The trains rush by like huge gigantic cans packed with human flesh, still undrained of blood" (p. 29). He thus exploits the tension between different stylistic levels by straddling and dissolving the boundary between the true and the mock epic.

The evocative description of the troop movements and confusion of the first days of World War I is rounded out by the small incident already mentioned: a poor Jew is saved from death by a signalman whose act, however, enrages the major in charge of a military train. And very soon the military machine will crush everyone—all the humble, the meek, the innocent and the awkward. The devil of the war has been unleashed.

This incident, which closes the fourth and final part of the Prodogue, plunges us in an epic manner into the midst of the story. At the start of Chapter I the railroad is appropriately described as an instrument of violence, violating the quiet and fragrant countryside on the outskirts of the world. The little railway station with its adjacent village bearing the long name of Topory-Czernielica is the microcosm of the book, and it forms a colorful setting for the opening chapters. The railroad provides the archetypal theme of the journey, both physical and spiritual, and also the dynamic element for whatever plot there is in the saga. The war and the railroad represent the dynamic motifs of the book. They develop against the static background of the stillness and passivity of the forgotten countryside living its own uneventful, primordial life. Wittlin juxtaposes the two elements in the very first sentences, affording us an example of his contrapuntal technique, whereby he contrasts and balances the different components and guides them toward a harmonious resolution.

Through forgotten corners of the Hucul countryside, where the smell of mint rises on summer nights, past dream-villages nestling in quiet pasture lands, where shepherds blow their long reed pipes, runs the train. It is the train, shut in between wooden fences, that alone links these quiet lands to the outer world. It stains the darkness with the dazzling glare of its headlight; it outrages the virgin stillness of the night's deep peace. The gleam of its lighted carriages tears through the veils of the mist; the long shriek of its whistle startles the hares, and wakens the sleepy curiosity of men. (p. 33)

V   *The Hero*

Likewise the humble protagonist Peter is introduced in contrast to the Viennese palaces and big cities mentioned in the

Prologue. The son of an unknown father and a very sketchily-described mother, Peter is forty-one years old. He is a porter at the station of Topory-Czernielica. He is not remarkable in any way except for the fact that he cannot read and write nor tell his right hand from his left—a motif which will recur with variations throughout the book.

The author who wisely remarks in the Prologue that he himself might have been a witness to the events he describes, uses Peter as a lens through which to observe the environment, to filter out truth from falsehood, exposing what masks itself as good and honorable but is actually evil and shameful. Through this filtration process we can focus our attention on phenomena which, although camouflaged to seem reasonable and human, are really inhuman, unreasonable and absurd. Thus the complex problem of the author's relationship to his work and his characters has been ingeniously solved, although at the same time another level of tension and contrast has been introduced—that between the highly sophisticated mind of the author and the naive consciousness of the illiterate Peter.

Wittlin has been taken to task for creating such a "homunculus" and such a "psychological riddle."[31] Other critics, like T. Breza, have seen in Peter Niewiadomski the author's *alter ego*—Peter's naive and primitive mind, his refreshing reactions to stereotyped situations and well-worn slogans being reminiscent of the poet's childlike heart. In this nontraditional novel Peter could be thought of as Everyman, groping his way through the darkness, unable to see the road ahead nor from which side disaster may strike him. Introducing Niewiadomski Wittlin says in the first Chapter: "Darkness was his home and his element, as water is the element of the fish, the earth is the element of the mole," and continues the simile on the "earthly" plane: . . . "like a mole, Peter worked in darkness and burrowed in subterranean passages essential to his well being. In the upper air he could only gasp desperately, like a fish out of water" (p. 34).

It is my contention that Peter Niewiadomski (the surname means son of an *unknown* [Italics mine Z. Y.] father), the unknown soldier, has been, as it were, unearthed by Wittlin who mocks the careful selection of the physical remains of some soldier by the dignitaries.[32] The novelist was not interested in Niewiadomski's physical appearance: it is described very sket-

chily (skull and hair . . .) only in Chapter 3 during his examination by the Draft Board. What did interest him was Peter's
dark, sylvan, primitive soul which feels affinity with everything
around it—the earth, the station, the cow in whose mooing he
recognizes his own pain. "His soul, too, was heavy and burdened and fed on grass" (p. 36). Here we may suspect the influence of Wittlin's early preoccupation with Expressionism, a
movement which favored retrogression to the primeval and liked
to contrast the primitive and natural against the corrupt, sophisticated and overcivilized.[33]

Regardless of whether earth-born Peter by origin was an earth
spirit or a graveyard apparition, Wittlin decided to reanimate
him, giving him "the flesh of the word" (in Julian Tuwim's
phrase). For this purpose Peter proved to be an almost ideal
epic hero; for he is inextricably immersed in his surroundings,
and literally implanted in his native soil and the station where
he has served for twenty years, to the point where one might
almost look upon him as a sort of human load-lifting crane.
Obscure, simple-minded, sincere, though not devoid of a certain
innate peasant slyness, and passive, he reflects faithfully the
topsy-turvy state of a world gone mad during the World War.
By introducing Peter as in part his own illiterate spokesman
Wittlin scored several important points concerning the technique
of the novel. He solved, at least partially, the important question
of *the point of view*[34] (italics mine, Z. Y.), assured the unity of
the work and discovered a way to write about the familiar
events of the war in a fresh and original manner.

VI *The Plot*

It is precisely this manner which is much more important
than the book's matter: the tension does not lie in the plot which
could be reduced to a single phrase, as was done by Alfred
Döblin, one of Wittlin's reviewers: "A Hucul signalman from
the station of Topory-Czernielica is drafted and spends his first
training days in a Hungarian training camp."[35] And yet, adds
Döblin, "there is tension in every figure, in every description."[36]
In a book on war one expects to find things like mobilization,
training, fighting, shooting, and facts which we know from history
and documentary materials. But the modern reader is not attracted by these already well-known facts but by their emotional,

lyrical and, more often, ironical aspects. He is interested in the irrational and associational workings of the mind, revealed or called to the surface by the writer's vision. The poetic intensity and artful simplicity of *The Salt of the Earth* make it a powerful mode of persuasion (a traditional prerogative of poetry) without the author's forcing his own ideology upon us. Composing his work more like a saga than a novel, Wittlin achieves an almost lyrical cohesion and compactness by using the associative principle of linking and interweaving the component parts. Various motifs—those of the Unknown Soldier, of War, of Death and the Devil—are combined to merge with, and overlay, each other. Minor motifs like those of Fear, of Treason, of the right and the left hand, follow suit reinforcing the already tight and condensed structure. The author achieves tension through subtly underscoring the main points of his vision by abundant ironies and ambiguities. Let us here examine how the writer sets about creating from the very beginning of the book the atmosphere of a world on its way out, using various motifs and devices, and replacing the dynamics of plot with the dynamics of style and language.

VII   *The War Comes to Topory-Czernielica*

The word "war" hits Peter suddenly: "War! The word crashed down on his head like a landslide. It pierced his cranium and passed through the membrane into his brain" (p. 46). And then "suddenly the word 'war' turned a somersault in his brain and dropped into his blood-stream, which would have burst, had not the blood swept the dread word back to his heart. From there it worked its way down into his belly, where it finished up with a pain as sharp and sudden as the stab of steel" (p. 46). If one were to examine this passage for its several ambiguities which all, incidentally, point in the direction of Doom, one might discern Peter's eventual fate even here. This impression is reinforced at the end of the chapter (note that because of their importance the opening and closing sections of chapters are skillfully linked together, both within each chapter and with each other) e. g., in Chapter 1 where the saws in the sawmill are "wailing"—a detail lost in translation—as if mourning Peter long before his girlfriend Magda and the other women of Topory-Czernielica will really lament for him in Chapter 6. Thus people and things are linked together as though they not only belonged to each other, but understood and knew one another.

The whole world as it is contained in microcosm in the life of a little station and the neighboring villages collapses over the heads of Peter and his boss the stationmaster when war is declared, and the train schedule, jokingly compared by the author to the Ten Commandments, is abolished by the General Staff. Along with all other pillars of peacetime existence it is completely overshadowed by the Declaration of War, around which the people, literate and illiterate alike, gather and recite "like the Litany in Church" (p. 50). "In these remote provinces belief in the Emperor Franz Josef united Roman Catholics and Greek Catholics, Jews and Armenians, in a common and universal Church" (p. 50). The theme of a sarcastic parallel between the Christian Church governed by God and the "church" governed by the Emperor is thus established early in the book to be continued, skillfully reinforced and underscored, down to the last two chapters where it becomes predominant. Thus the new man-made myths are scrutinized and set off against the old beliefs so as to better expose their true nature.

Peter, too, worships the Emperor and has long dreamt of being awarded a uniform cap with the Emperor's monogram, the official token of recognition for his devoted service to the station. His dream comes true in an ironic fashion when the war breaks out and the stationmaster has to replace the signalman at signal-box No. 86, who has been drafted. Now the war is on, and ordinary values are reversed: ". . . . this unexpected and conditional promotion was almost a humiliation" (p. 52). Another allusion to Peter's impending doom may be found at the end of the chapter. Unfortunately, it has become lost in translation. The sentence should read: "Peter has lost his head completely since he began wearing the imperial cap on it" instead of "And the imperial cap he now wore could not prevent Peter from losing his head" (p. 54). A subtly sinister subtext underlying *The Salt of the Earth,* which every detail reflects as a whole, seems to constitute the hidden "soul" of the plot right from the start of the saga.

The blessed stillness of the countryside which was first disturbed at the beginning of the book by the railroad is now also being disturbed by the Emperor whose summons to his soldiers reaches the remotest corners of the Empire. "The Emperor's own voice could not reach to the Hucul land, but the Imperial Post could reach it, and where even the Post broke down the gendarmes and the district clerks took over the task" (p. 55). The Emperor summons "both the living and the dead," (p. 54) since the registers of the "omniscient" military authorities are quite outdated. Again the mocking parallel between God and Emperor is discreetly alluded to.

VIII   *The Call to Arms*

The summons to the army, stylized in epic form, is projected sarcastically onto a universal plane: "Once in his life every man must report for service. For the army, as for the Kingdom of Heaven, all are called, but not all are chosen" (p. 66). "Every man" here is most immediately Peter Niewiadomski. On a quiet and beautiful summer evening Peter is visited by a gendarme, whom Wittlin presents in a manner reminiscent of Homer as the personification of war:

Something was moving in the stillness, some one was coming to the box. . . . And the danger, like a poisonous snake, wound softly through the bushes, gleamed golden against the grass, disappeared again and finally slid into the open. . . . Down in the bushes a bayonet flashed and glinted, catching and mirroring the rays of the setting sun. Then the brass spike of a helmet appeared. And suddenly War came over to the embankment. It strolled along in black, hobnailed boots; it climbed the steps with its sword and rifle, and presented itself to Peter Niewiadomski in the guise of the corporal of the *gendarmerie*, Jan Durek. (pp. 57-58)

In Polish this passage is saturated with alliterations, verb repetitions and other sound and light effects which make it particularly expressive. The war marches down on Peter and others like him disguised not as the Greek Pallas Athena but as one of the lesser "gods" of the contemporary world, that is in the uniform of an Austrian gendarme. Despite his significant name (Durek means "stupid"), this gendarme is clever enough to be able to mock the naive Peter who cannot detect the irony of metaphoric speech. The fact of Peter's illiteracy gives the gendarme an aura of special power. He reads the mobilization order to Peter "like an actor reading the death sentence in a play" (p. 62). And to complete his triumph and Peter's discomfiture he adds curtly:

"And do you know how they treat deserters nowadays? Court-martial and a bullet in the head" (p. 63). The vision of Peter's possible future fate again confronts us, though the motifs of treason and desertion will appear only later in the book.

The health examination given Peter by the local Draft Board (cf. Chapter 3) is stylized by Wittlin like the Last Judgment. Here men's bodies are weighed and measured and duly marked (like those of animals destined for slaughter) with a blue pencil. But in contrast to the Last Judgment in this case all are damned: "And now these chairs had become Stations of the Cross for the damned, as though the Last Judgment admitted of one sentence only: Hell" (p. 77). From the moment Peter answers "here" when his name is called by the sergeant-major, "the word, the written word, the word that had wandered through books and registers, became flesh" (p. 74). The parallel between God and Emperor, between the real and the false creation of the "new" man for the sake not of life in Christ, but "life" (for which read: "death") in the Emperor, is reinforced by skillful repetition. Thus as soon as Peter had been assigned unjustifiably to category "A," his name, "the *word* was already transformed into the body of a soldier with a regimental number" (Italics mine, Z. Y.) (p. 98). Dr. Jellinek, the surgeon-major who certifies Peter for service in spite of his weak heart is "the accredited intermediary between the Emperor and Death" (p. 97). Death reigns supreme throughout the entire chapter. Indeed, it becomes a dual phenomenon: both civil death and the "military one which destroys perfectly healthy organisms." Wittlin refers to the subjects of the medical examination as a "ring of ghosts" and a "ghost circus." With magnificent artistic consistency he equips the examination room with "two large trestles, looking . . . like two bodies of horses with the heads and tails cut off . . ." and a number of iron bars with black iron weights on each end, the size of human heads" (pp. 99-100). The sinister meaning behind these details becomes apparent a little later when, having taken the bodies of future soldiers *individually,* the Emperor binds their souls to him with an oath administered, this time *collectively* (Italics mine, Z. Y.) in an obviously mock ceremony, in the course of which God is reduced to "an endless series of naughts added to the highest possible numeral, the Emperor" (p. 104) and a mock Holy Ghost presides over the ceremony in the guise not "of a white dove, but a black, double-headed eagle. The crooked talons gripped convulsively round an iron bar with a black ball at each end of it" (p. 105). Now the implied meaning of the iron weights "the size of human heads" becomes more apparent. In this passage the author's irony is directed against the Emperor who deals in bodies and souls; for it is the individual soul which should be treasured most and handled *individually,* not collectively. The Emperor, however, is interested in the soldiers' *bodies,* not their *souls;* he gives the former individual treatment, taking their souls *collectively.* (Italics mine, Z. Y.) But in Wittlin's view, everything has a soul, even trees. (Cf. the poem "The Pain of a Tree," analyzed in Chapter I.) Peter, who is closely linked to the earth is still capable of rebelling against the inhuman procedure to which he is subjected by the Emperor's minions: "Revolt rioted in Peter's body. It mounted from the leaden feet which seemed so embedded in the ground that an effort was needed to uproot them. It rose from the tough horny soles; it welled out from under his toe-nails and rushed upwards, mighty and untamed . . . ." (p. 94).

However this revolt collapses beneath the impact of fear. "Revolt drew back horror-stricken at its own power and returned to the earth whence it had come" (p. 94). Here we can almost feel Peter's "rustling," his comments on things he cannot comprehend and combat, complaining like the tree in Wittlin's poem. He is an amalgam of humility, helplessness, ignorance and sin, instinctively feeling his way through the dark tunnels of earth. Thus Wittlin can switch the focus of his composition freely back and forth between Peter as the allegorical type of a humble human being, and the universal and symbolic plane. He can end Chapter 2, in which Peter does not eat his supper after the gendarme's visit, with a generalization: "Over the whole world gendarmes were spoiling people's appetites" (p. 69), or conclude a chapter in the style of a collective Last Judgment with a line where the focus reverts abruptly to Peter: "Thus Peter Niewiadomski swore the oath to the Emperor" (p. 105).

IX   *"The End of the World"*

Epic stylization is sometimes even more pronounced; for example at the beginning of Chapter 4, which reads: "For as long as one could remember, blind organ-grinders at annual fairs in the market places had been predicting the end of the world. But that this day of God's wrath should fall precisely on the 21st of August, 1914—that no one expected, not the wisest in Topory-Czernielica, not in all Galicia" (p. 107). But Wittlin, who never forgets that his epic is a modern one verging on a mock epic, a work which must synthesize the tragedy and comedy which are so inseparably linked together in the lives of modern men, immediately brings in incidental characters for comic relief. Thus we are told in an ironic tone of the Priest Makarucha's reflections on the theme of the end of the world. Again, as at the beginning of the book, our microcosm, the station of Topory-Czernielica becomes the focal point; this time to show the advance of enemy troops and the invasion of fear into Topory, and more especially into Peter Niewiadomski's soul (p. 115). His instinctive fear is justified: the gendarme Durek has intruded into the summer stillness of the countryside in order to take over signal box No. 86, the one which Peter has come to love, and to bring him orders to depart for Hungary the very next day. Here one can observe an interesting parallel between the fate of the little station, to which Peter is so inseparably attached, and his own fate. No sooner has Topory-Czernielica been elevated to the status of a "military base" than it has to lose its head, its symbol of identity, when Peter has to take down the signboard. Peter's promotion to the post of signalman ends with a dangerous journey into the unknown. He feels guileless and helpless in the face of strange, unfamiliar powers. In the near future he too may be left like the little station "without a name, without a head, without a soul" (p. 137). He feels himself to be in the Devil's power. "He had the sensation that he was being delivered over to the Devil" (p. 122). Hitherto he was geared to life in a little station where no one knew his handicap—his inability to distinguish between right and left. But now "he felt that it would come to light sooner or later; the Devil would see to that. Some day it would bring terrible disaster upon him. Would it then come from the right or from the left? Who could say?" (p. 122). The motif of the Devil which appears early in the book resounds more and more clearly as the book proceeds. It is usually coupled with the War motif. Peter, who with his naive questions and reactions is always harking back to the claims of reality embarrasses the gendarme who comes to take

over the signal-box by inquiring how far the Russian armies
have advanced. The gendarme, well-versed in official reports,
recites the official lie about "Russians . . . retreating all along
the line" (p. 126). It makes Peter wonder whether it was not
the Devil himself who "was leading astray the whole Imperial
and Royal Army, making it think it was advancing, when really
it was retreating further and further" (p. 127). Here, in a manner
half-serious and half-jesting which Wittlin veils with his light
touch, we are given a vision of the absurdities of the world,
especially those of a world at war. But at bottom the author is
serious about the motif of the Devil and Peter's peasant beliefs
are treated half humorously mainly for the sake of diverting the
reader.

This is especially obvious in Chapter 6 which deals with the
death of the Pope and the solar eclipse, an eclipse which the inhabitants of Topory take as signalling the real, imminent end
of the world. In trying to understand the world around him,
which has become less and less intelligible since the outbreak
of war, Peter comes up with excellent explanations of the dark
powers, of the Pope's death and the "pall of darkness" which has
come over the earth. Does the pacifist Pius X who wanted to
"renew everything in Christ" (p. 147) die because "the clergy
now allow killing?" (p. 154). Is not Christendom without a
Pope like a man without a head? "Now the Devil will run wild"
(p. 157). The best explanation Peter can think of is that "the
Devil had robbed God of the whole of the fifth commandment,
and had sold it to the Emperor" (p. 157). This is another piece
of Wittlin's private mythology. The Devil reigning supreme and
the death of the Pope are connected by Peter with the eclipse
of the sun and are stylized as the end of the world, which he
expresses in quasi-biblical, quasi-folk tale language. But Peter
goes one step further: he connects the solar eclipse not only
with war and with the death of the Holy Father but with his
own sins, for his faith in the soul is strong. Together with the
other Huculs he prays for forgiveness in the face of this "darkness at noon" and receives forgiveness: "The Creator gave a
favorable hearing to the prayers of the poor Huculs, and for
the last time He forgave the sinful world" (p. 162). One hears
in this passage the accents of a parody of Wittlin's own youthful

utopianism when he believed he could save the world with his poems—prayers.

It is the motif of Death and the Devil, not that of an even temporary salvation, which is central to this chapter, and this chapter is central to the book. The real end of the world, the little world of Peter and those like him cannot be averted, even by the solar eclipse; they must part with their native land and journey toward a menacing future. On the surface the end of the chapter describes the entrainment of the *Landsturm* headed for Hungary but at a deeper level it depicts the takeover by death, here skillfully blended and linked with the departure scene. Wittlin knows how to overshadow the living soldiers as they are departing with "heads of unknown corporals, sergeant-majors, captains," which "again and again loomed up out of nothingness, crawled out from under the ground, sprang up from the gravel, and from the rails, and jumped out from the telegraph poles"[37] (p. 155). What a background for Wittlin's "unknown soldier," the soldier who is now beginning the journey from which there will be for him no return except in an epic song!

His fate is heralded by the lamentations described so poignantly in Chapter 6 where "two Jewesses mourned like the leaders of a Greek chorus" and "the Hucul women joined in with the whine of whipped bitches; babies whimpered and dogs howled" (p. 173). The expressiveness of the scene is enhanced by the use of a simile. "The train pushed straight through all this human grief and despair, as in winter it pushed through the snowdrifts" (p. 173). A dynamic allegorical personification of death reinforces the impression. "Without the formality of a platform-ticket death strolled unconcernedly over the whole station of Topory-Czernielica, blowing its cold breath down the neck, first of one man, then of another" (p. 170). Two laments provide a frame for the chapter: the first for the death of the Pope, the other for the departing soldiers. A concealed note of mourning is also to be found in the lyrical description of Peter's preparations for the journey when he takes with him a piece of bread from the Mother-Earth and also the key to his house, to which he is not to return. No one doubts that the rails (the image of the railroad serves to move the plot forward) do not lead to the world of life as before but "only to war, the straight road to death" (p. 174). As the train progresses (Chapter 7) into the unknown mythical Hungary where people gobble paprika (cf. the lotus eaters in *The Odyssey!*) the laments of women, "this universal language of pain" (see the Prologue) accompany it at every station, while invisible hands feed the human fuel into the ovens of war.

X *The Journey*

The worst kind of estrangement, not only from home but from one's self, begins during this journey, where all the values are now reversed. Peter's tender feelings for the railroad which he has served so faithfully for almost twenty of his forty years change to wrath. It no longer has the charm of distant lands, it no longer serves life; it has become a slave of the war, feeding the army with beef and the war with "cannon fodder." Instead of praying with the others, as he did in the previous chapter, in an attempt to avert the end of the world, he now curses the railway and soon, together with his fellows, he will curse his own mother for giving him the life of which he is no longer master. Uprooted from his native soil and from his station, Peter becomes selfish and suspicious, estranged even from his own "folk" who are riding on the same transport. They are now in an alien country, where the Emperor for some unknown reason is only a King (like a split-personality of the Lord of War) and where people speak some unintelligible language "as hot as paprika."

It was as if the Emperor wanted to mix up the languages as had once been done at the Tower of Babel. The Devil himself, disguised as a Hungarian gendarme, refused to let "our people" (as Wittlin calls the Huculs in the Biblical manner) drink water from an allegedly contaminated well. This incited the thirsty recruits to start rioting. The well, an eternal symbol of love and life, (especially in Slavic folklore) becomes a source of hatred between the Galician and Hungarian soldiers, subjects of the same sovereign: Franz Josef. True, later they quench their thirst with wine and achieve some mode of communication with each other, but that wine conveys the epic connotation of blood, the blood they will all shed in the future.

As the physical and spiritual journey of Peter and the others goes on his attitudes change; he begins to call things by their true names and no longer tries to rationalize about God and the

Emperor. Until now a loyal subject of Franz Josef, he begins to
understand that the oath he swore to the Emperor "was pledging
the whole of one's life, as it were, and a man had but one life"
(p. 181). In order to solve this problem Peter wishes he had two
lives: one which he could give for the Emperor while keeping
the other for himself and a safe return home. But instead of this
ideal solution it is the loss of his one real life for the Emperor
which seems more and more probable. Peter is gradually preparing to undergo a complete reversal of all his former values;
to lose his faith in justice and his innocence.

Wittlin dramatizes these changes. He makes Peter witness a
reverse eclipse of the sun at the brightly-lit station in Budapest
where midnight appeared like broad daylight: "No, this wasn't
night: the Army has abolished night. This was broad daylight"
(p. 199). It is a topsy-turvy world, a "devil's vaudeville" (to use
Dostoevsky's expression) in which everything occurs the wrong
way around. Peter soon falls into a dream where he hears a
succession of sounds—a veritable trans-sense language—which
soon changes into a primeval language which he is able to understand. His naive primitive consciousness is now completely intact
only in dreams. The dream seems prophetic: Peter falls down
beneath the weight of a crown which Father Makarucha puts
on his head: it is the Holy Crown of St. Stephen!

XI   *The Training Camp*

The training camp in Andrasfalva, Hungary, described in
Chapter 8, is a world apart, isolated by barbed wire, and symbolically located next to a slaughter house and a cemetery. The
account of "our folks'" reactions to their new surroundings is one
of the most vivid parts of the whole book. In Andrasfalva they
become totally alienated from themselves and from their own
countrymen in the camp who had been called up earlier. The
newly arrived "sons of the Hucul earth" (again Wittlin refers to
them in a Biblical manner) are unable to recognize even their
"own folk" who have undergone a startling metamorphosis in
this bewildering camp. Wittlin, a master of the important satirical
device of metamorphosis and grotesque distortion[38] has the untrained and uninitiated "old shaggy draftees"[39] witness a veritable
devil's trick. He brings before their, and our, startled eyes a
moving battalion which resembles a "living ribbon of grey-blue

cloth," a "huge resounding wall" (p. 213), anything in a word,
but the living people, their "own folk," whom they knew back
at home. . . . "They all began to realize that this display . . . had
some deep and secret meaning, that it was something more than
human, although produced by human feet" (p. 213). While
appreciating the unearthly beauty of the march "they shrank
back in alarm from the invisible powers, which, no doubt, would
transform them also into moving walls" (p. 215). Wittlin knows
how to condense the atmosphere of fear, impending doom and
diabolism in his description of this "death camp" whose atmosphere seems to foreshadow the even more terrible camps of
World War II. Terror governs the camp and plagues the souls
of its inhabitants. "Terror will one day lead forth these disciplined
formations . . . out of Hungary, and hunt them to their death"
(p. 218). This terror is compared to gas. An invisible "zone of
danger" lies between the soldiers and the rest of the world, "across
which no one dared step—neither from the one side nor the
other" (p. 217-218). This recalls the division between the living
and the dead in the Scriptures.[40] In the camp even lighter moments are permeated with an ironic sobriety: When the hungry
new arrivals are fed, they are given meat usually reserved for
festive occasions like Easter. However, since all normal values
have been reversed by the army, one might well suspect that
they have been issued meat rations so that they in turn can be
used as fodder in the fight against the enemy. The meat menu in
the army is not connected with Easter or Resurrection, but rather
with impending death! (This impression is skillfully reinforced
by similes and metaphors like "cannon fodder," "soldier's meat,"
or "kilograms of human bodies"—a device already used in the
Prologue.)

While eating his first army soup Peter suddenly sees before
him an apparition of his dead mother who had once saved his
life by feeding him some kind of barley soup. . . . Applying the
remnants of his naive, direct insight Peter draws a parallel and
asks himself the question: "Perhaps Imperial soup did protect
from death? . . . And it was for this reason that the Emperor
fed his soldiers, his children with it? . . ." (p. 228). However his
naïveté is replaced by irony, the irony which appears even in
his relationship to the Emperor whom he still loves but now is
beginning to distrust. Remembering the words of the War Proc-

lamation which touched him so much at the time of the outbreak of the war: "My dear peoples . . ." Peter thinks—"He had a nice way of showing his affection . . ." (p. 244). He is now ready to bury his innocence together with others of "our folk" who all lose their innocence during their first army camp night when they are ". . . cursing their mothers" (p. 249) and are disappointed by earth and sky" (p. 248). The poisoned air in the camp of Andrasfalva prepares the "sons of the Hucul earth" for their incorporation into the army and submission to military discipline: to question nothing and to keep silent (the prerogative of the dead). Wittlin compares this absorption into the army with initiation into the Eleusinian mysteries; i. e., a "communion with death" which takes place on earth (p. 234). Thus the new deity called Subordination (capitalized in the original though not in the English translation) emerges into full light. She will demand submission, veneration and even human sacrifice.[41]

Almost simultaneously the high priest of this new deity (at the outset of the twentieth century people were searching for new myths with as much eagerness as today's generation), Regimental Sergeant-Major Rudolph Bachmatiuk, Chief Instructor of an Imperial and Royal Regiment of Galician Infantry, takes over the destinies of the newly-arrived recruits, displacing Peter from the center of our attention. The two last chapters of the book are mainly devoted to Bachmatiuk. He is the embodiment of the fear and terror which dominate the camp. He represents the abstract idea of military service; he is a perfect tool for supplying the army with what it needs: "human products," soldiers versed in all the arcana of the military art, the art which Bachmatiuk cultivates." It is he who greets each new batch of recruits with the ominous threat: "I will make men out of you," thus annulling their creation by God in His image and their coming into the world as the sons of earthly mothers. . . .

His words held terrible power. When he shouted: "I shall make a man of you!" the poor creature who heard him felt that he was in the presence of a veritable Creator. He felt that soon shocking, monstrous things were about to happen, primeval things, things of the Apocalpse; that Creation was only now about to begin. God the Father counted no longer, for the brown, hairy finger of the Regimental Sergeant-Major exuded a current which could kill all living things, and then again call them back to life. (p. 269)

In Chapter 10 we see for ourselves the effect of his words: Peter, who would like to lift his hand and cross himself, is unable to do so: his hand felt as though it were glued to the seam of his trousers. Bachmatiuk, ironically stylized as a priest of a new deity Subordination, a person living in a "cell" and seeking to achieve a mystical communion "with the holy spirit of duty" (p. 265), presents Wittlin's prophetic vision of the totalitarian-type soldier. Bachmatiuk will not hesitate to bring human victims as offerings to the deity he serves—one which is ". . . more horrible and powerful than the officers . . . even more mighty than the Emperor, more mighty even than death" (p. 218). Serving his deity he breeds fear and hatred both at first and at second-hand—"chewing out" his subordinates who in turn take it out on their inferiors. Thus the first real enemy of the newly-arrived recruits turns out to be their own corporal who wants to take revenge on them for the punishment he has received from Bachmatiuk.

The motif of ambiguity as to who is one's friend and who one's enemy is sounded discreetly throughout the book. All the lines of Wittlin's skillful construction converge on Bachmatiuk: he exists to lay bare the final absurdity of the myth of war and "war-like deeds" which has already been exposed in Peter's conscious-ness. The new "saint" of the new Church Militant of the Emperor in himself illustrates its deceitful nature. He will never practice what he preaches: he will never go to the front; for he has be-come irreplaceable in the job of coaching others in all the 37 Articles of War—of the new faith—the ones that teach men how to kill and so how to break God's commandments. Thus he trans-forms the new faith into an absurdity and is but the last of a long line of characters in *The Salt of the Earth* who send others to die without exposing themselves to danger. This line begins with Franz Josef, the Supreme Commander who is fighting only against the deteriorating blood of the House of Habsburg, con-tinues with Peter's boss the stationmaster and then goes to the commanding officer Lieutenant Leithuber, whose right hand withered long ago in the senseless military service but who is still convinced that he has the power to send people to their deaths while commanding with his left. The Evangelical motif of the right and the left hand acquires a new significance in connection with Peter, serving, like many other devices, to contrast the "old"

Christian faith with the "new faith" of the "brethren in the Emperor. . . ."

This parodistic juxtaposition reaches its zenith in the last chapter where the counterfeit creator Bachmatiuk finally achieves a moment of supreme triumph and sees his efforts crowned with success; "new men" for the needs of the Army have been created out of "our folk." "In the beginning there was the Word: the Word that stilled the waves; the Word that was followed by the stillness of Death. Bachmatiuk stood with half-closed eyes, like a music-lover at a symphony concert. He drew himself up to his full height, and in tones like a crowning cockerel, gave the order. 'Attention!'" (p. 313). He read to the newly-uniformed soldiers from his "Holy Writ"—the 37 Articles of War: . . . "Enraptured, Bachmatiuk gazed upon the frozen faces, and the uniforms, and the boots. He was soothed by the ideal stillness engendered by his word. He breathed in the sweet odor of obedience and fear, and was content. On this first day of creation, as he took possession of the souls of the last class of the *Landsturm,* he saw his work completed. And he knew that it was good" (p. 314). A parallel to the Book of Genesis immediately comes to mind.

In the last two chapters which are completely dominated by Bachmatiuk Peter Niewiadomski eclipses him only once, in a single brief but poignant scene which takes place in an old Magyar brewery now used as a storehouse for old uniforms and ammunition. It is a ghost scene when the spirits of those who have been killed, which according to a Hucul legend still linger in the barrels of the old rifles, come before Peter and offer him "long grains of lead" which they drew out of their "torn breasts, heads and bellies." "Peter grew frightened, and decided that the Magyar brewers, Farkas and Gjormeky, were not brewers at all, but were devils, and that they had kept here not beer, sound beer made from hops and barley, but blood" (p. 300).[42]

Peter still possesses a soul. However, thanks to Bachmatiuk's exertions he is being transformed into a soldier with no need for a soul—without which he will make an even better soldier. He is rapidly approaching the final stage of his preparation to be absorbed by the Army, body and soul. He is being given a "reeking outfit" (p. 302) which "dedicated him to death" (p. 302), the imperial uniform, an "official wrapping" in which killing has been sanctioned not only by the Army but even by the Church.

The parodistic parallel between the Christian Church and the "Church Militant" of Franz Josef which is discreetly drawn throughout the book ends with Bachmatiuk who is exposed as a counterfeit creator. Bachmatiuk evaluates his work of robbing human beings of their souls, of that Divine element which, according to the Christian viewpoint, is the mystical core of human personality, as good. Wittlin's destruction of the war myth is complete. Living according to a "New Writ," Service Regulations Nos. 1, 2 and 3, by this "Bible of Order, the only order in this vale of sorrows . . ." (p. 270), means just this: living in order to bring death to others and to accept death for oneself. On page 270 the unwittingly macabre death scheme neatly sums up "the entire aspect of mortality" within the framework of army regulations.

CHAPTER 5

The Salt of the Earth: *Observations on Style*

THE condensed account of *The Salt of the Earth* given in the previous chapter was aimed especially at the non-Polish reader with a view to exposing him more closely to the author's vision and preparing him for a discussion of certain questions dealing more specifically with the formal, stylistic aspect of the book. The question of genre in Wittlin's prose work has been touched on before (cf. Chapter 4). Granting that *The Salt of the Earth* is a "novel," though a novel "with a difference," we may apply to it a traditional, if now somewhat antiquated analysis in terms of plot (or action), background (or setting), characters, dialogue and style. Even though Wittlin knows how to create and preserve here the appearance of a novel, we know already that it has virtually no plot. It could even be read more or less as a historical novel. Some of its personages are indeed historical (Franz Josef and his aides), while others are fictional (Leithuber, Bachmatiuk, Dr. Jellinek, Magda), with the main figure, Peter, being half-historical (in his capacity as an Unknown Soldier), and half-fictional (as the porter or keeper of signal box No. 86).

I *The Characters and the Setting*

As for the problems of the characters and the setting or background of the book, it is difficult to decide here who or what is the hero and who or what forms the background. Peter Niewiadomski is in such close communion with his natural environment that he and the other Huculs whose presence we feel are virtually inseparable from it. Peter's status in the chain of being is very low: he is somewhere on the borderline between men, animals, plants or even inanimate objects (he is compared by the author to a railroad station crane or to a piece of furniture). Could not Peter and the other Huculs be thought of as a kind of setting, a background against which historical events are projected by the author? Is not the chief conflict of the book between the earth (and everything which is on it and which grows out of it) and war—the cataclysm which fatally affects this earth?

It is clear that the peaceful, idyllic countryside and its people are contrasted with the intrusion of evil forces which threaten everyone's life and well-being. Using what Ruskin called "the pathetic fallacy,"[1] personification and other poetic devices, Wittlin succeeds in creating in Topory-Czernielica a microcosm, endowed with its own soul, a veritable character in the book, no less a living being than the others. When we come to problems of style we will discover that Wittlin writes this book as a poet, not as a realistic writer. However, since *The Salt of the Earth* has the surface appearance of a "realistic" novel, the critics approached it from this angle precisely. Some even took the trouble to point out various factual inaccuracies in the work: for example, that there is no such place as Topory-Czernielica or that the Hucui land begins not in Snyatin, as Wittlin says, but from the mountain border: i.e., from Sokolowka behind Kosow.[2] Such critics apparently did not realize that Wittlin is not concerned with the authenticity of any specific locality. He is fond of so-called "word mythology," and in this case he combined the two names Topory and Czernielica simply in order to play with them for his own artistic purposes. Here is how he accounts for the origin of the half-mythical, half-geographical place: "The world was full of names, names that sprang up like the wild flowers in the fields. God himself had sown them centuries before. There were soft, sweet-smelling names, and others that were sharp, and harsh, and sullen. How, for example, did Topory get the name 'Topory'?" ("Topory" is the Polish word for "axes.") Probably at one time there had been nothing there but forests, and the woodcutters had come with axes to cut down the trees" (pp. 134-35). Characteristically, Topory-Czernielica is most frequently described in terms of odors, "the eternal reek of country homes . . . a mixture of wood smoke, cheese, whey, poultry droppings, and *poverty*" (p. 139; italics mine, Z. Y.) In Wittlin's poetics smell is of tremendous importance: not only does it characterize material objects, but abstract concepts are also capable of producing smells. Topory-Czernielica is also characterized by its stillness, described by Wittlin in several lyrical passages (lyricism often accompanies the image of Peter as well as that of the countryside). Here is one such passage, which describes not merely the outward impression of stillness itself, but, one might say, the very soul of stillness:

And now the hour had come. Not dark, but light, being the hour before the night falls, the hour when the earth grows still, as though stroked by the hand of her for whom the bells of all the churches were ringing at that moment. A clear sky, blue as the robe of the Blessed Virgin, softly enfolded the earth where noise and strife were dying down. The very insects, weary of endless circling in the warm air, had muffled their buzzing wings. At that hour human hearts, full of turmoil, beat more quietly, and to the most brutal there was granted the blessing of peace. (p. 56)[3]

In peacetime the stillness might be disturbed only by the crickets, one of which is likened by the music-loving Wittlin to "that Mozart of peasant hearths" (p. 145).

With the intrusion of war all is changed. The war's impact is reflected, for example, in the scene where the signboard of the station is removed by Peter. Even the illiterate Peter thinks of the double name of the station as of its first name and surname (p. 135). "To rob the station of its signboard was just the same as robbing a man of his name" (p. 134). The station is no more. Only a building remains: "without a name, without a head, without a soul" (p. 137). The Earth itself, the peaceful and idyllic countryside with all its burden of the living and the dead can be considered a personage as well as a setting. Wittlin uses it as a contrasting image to that of the War. This opposition between the Earth and the War provides that conflict between opposing forces, which more often than not forms the so-called "action" in a "regular" novel. In an attempt to name the hidden, evil forces we arrive at the following personified forces: War, the Devil, and Death; three things that are so much interwoven and interconnected in the book. But can we also regard these three as personages?

The War, the historical event on which Wittlin focuses his attention, is portrayed by him with such vividness and plasticity that it assumes the shape of a real protagonist. As has already been noted by Fryde,[4] it first appears as an allegory in the Prologue of the book; with its birth being strikingly depicted in other sections as well. War is personified; it is even accompanied by the old symbol of evil—the snake. We notice this with the first appearance of Corporal Durek (pp. 56-57) and we see it also in the comparison of the war telegrams to snake coils (p. 48 *et al.*). We see the encroachment of war upon everything and everybody, its dynamic development, its sweeping over places and people alike, its "life" which in the two later volumes of the trilogy is to end in its "death," the date of which we know from history. . . . The War is afforded a more thorough treatment in the book than are other characters who are here not portrayed from birth to death, as is often done in novels.

Wittlin has succeeded not only in creating the "body" of a half-mythical village but its soul too. Similarly, he has depicted the war and even the time when it broke out, the drought-stricken summer of 1914, in such a way that it could well qualify as another hero of the book.

Wittlin's prose has the compactness of poetry. Every component is related to other components; all details eventually converge to compose a portrait or convey some symbolic meaning. To cite but one example, we have a symbolic leitmotif beginning in Chapter 2, where in the breaking of the cows' voices one can hear "the anticipation of the slaughterhouse" (p. 69). In Chapter 4 a parallel between cows and human mothers is convincingly drawn. In Chapter 8 Peter's Training Post is significantly located near a slaughterhouse. In Chapter 9 the Training Post is replaced without a comment by a slaughterhouse! . . . The density of Wittlin's prose, where every thread reinforces the texture, adding another link to the total continuity, makes it difficult to distinguish between the more and the less important elements in the book, or to define precisely the nature of his craftsmanship.

How does he, for instance, achieve his effects in revealing to us the psychological depths of a human soul? What about the characterizations, aside from the fact that they are so close to his background? Despite the fact that the two principal "heroes," Peter Niewiadomski and Rudolph Bachmatiuk, could well be regarded as personified ideas at almost every turn of the book, their primary importance being as instruments to expose the absurdity of the institution of war from two opposed vantage points: that of one who knows nothing about war and that of one who knows all about it; they can also be seen, especially

Bachmatiuk, as splendid character studies. They show the keenness of the author's observation and a fine insight into human or, in Bachmatiuk's case, inhuman nature. The latter has been drawn (overdrawn, perhaps) with masterful and prophetic strokes. The Bachmatiuks served in all armies not only in World War I but also in World War II with still more disastrous results.

We would need to quote at great length to show how Wittlin has succeeded in depicting the "body" and the "soul" of the supposedly soulless sergeant. To do this he has used various techniques: direct description and also many forms of indirect description; the reader, for example, has an opportunity to deduce the personality from its setting—Bachmatiuk's room is stylized as a cell with a picture of Captain Knauss, his dead superior, in place of an icon. To make Bachmatiuk's image still more indelible, Wittlin introduces at the beginning of Chapter 9 a witty parallel between him and the clock which "shook in harsh but impotent obedience against its own spring" (p. 251). Bachmatiuk is also characterized by his clothes and his behavior. Wittlin does not avoid, however, pointing out certain puzzling aspects of the sergeant's personality, which do not quite fit in with his "straight" role as a model soldier. We wonder why Bachmatiuk gets drunk on Sundays and leaves the Regiment unattended; he, the slave and devoted servant of the Deity known as Subordination. Why does Bachmatiuk, who is unthinkable out of uniform, own civilian clothes? Does he suffer—he who brings suffering to so many other people? Does he suffer and grow older because he must prepare candidates for corpses in his job of "making new men," or merely because he loves order above all else and cannot stand the least taint of disorder? Wittlin wisely holds in reserve the right to tell us more about him later.

The soul of Peter, the "Unknown Soldier," proves even more enigmatic than Bachmatiuk's, despite the fact that Peter is apparently a simpleton. Why, for instance, does he love the Emperor so much? (The Freudian-oriented critic might speak here of the "father-image," which could also explain certain features in Bachmatiuk and even the stationmaster.) Will he stay true to his oath or will fear—a motive elaborated on in the book—drive him to desertion? In any case, as we have already seen, the myth of the heroic soldier dying for his Fatherland has been more than once shown up for the nullity it is.

What else did Wittlin achieve by portraying the "soul" (Bach-matiuk) and the "body" (Peter) of a regiment, a microcosm of the Austro-Hungarian Army? By making them both non-Austrian (Bachmatiuk is Ukrainian, Peter half-Ukrainian, half-Polish) and assigning them to a regiment "commanded" in peacetime by a Balkan king with whom Franz Josef is now at war, a glaring light was thrown upon the "integrity" of the regiment and per-haps even of the whole Austrian military system. We hope to find answers to all these questions in the continuation of the trilogy.

If we examine even more closely the two "heroes" of *The Salt of the Earth* we cannot help observing a certain resemblance between them which is not, perhaps, at first apparent. They are both depicted as visionaries—Peter despite his dumbness, Bach-matiuk despite his stiffness. Both like things more than people: Peter finds it hard to part from the things he loves; to Bach-matiuk a uniform is much more precious than a man, and "how much more a rifle . . ." (p. 299). Peter loves the sound of words so much that he is prone to judge people by the sound of their names, notwithstanding what he may hear about them. Bach-matiuk does not simply give an order; he "sings" it, half closing his eyes "like a music lover at a symphony concert" (p. 313). If we can detect a trace of self-parody when Wittlin makes Peter's prayers save the world during the solar eclipse, Bach-matiuk too, is used by the author for purposes of self-parody. In his act of counterfeit creation at the end of the book we cannot help noticing the author's joy over the success of his work—the joy of an artificer, who has imposed form upon living matter. We may speculate that while Wittlin-the dreamer, Wittlin-the nature lover, Wittlin-the lyricist participated in the making of Peter, it was Wittlin the stern artificer, one of those uncom-promising creators called "inhuman" by Jung,[5] who went into the making of Bachmatiuk, although finding continuities between the author's ego and that of his heroes is hardly rewarding.

It is interesting to note that in his depiction of characters Witt-lin does not use linguistic characterization and deliberately avoids dialogue. Dialogue, which for a novelist is "an oppor-tunity to suggest continuity between his fictional world and the real world,"[6] as the perceptive critic David Lodge has written, is absent from Wittlin's book. Apparently, he deliberately chose not to avail himself of the "opportunity."

However, in *The Salt of the Earth* we do have an "interior monologue" of Peter. It contains Peter's rationalizations concerning God and the Emperor:

> Everything on this earth belongs either to the Emperor or to God, reflected Peter. Earth and sky, the Pruth, the Czeremosz, and the Carpathians, and cows and dogs, and man belong to God. All the railways, on the other hand, all the cars and engines, all signal-boxes and gates, down to a rusty bit of wire, down to a rotten tie under the rails, belong to the Emperor. To steal a tie is to injure the Emperor, and for that the Imperial gendarme takes people to an Imperial prison. And quite right. And, of course, the chief thing on this earth is money. And to whom does money belong? It belongs to him whose head is engraved on it. The Emperor gives men money, just as God gives them life. Money and life are just loans. The Emperor is a partner of God. Therefore, he has the right to a man's life, which is only lent to him by God.
> (p. 65)

This internal monologue contains several features of linguistic characterization which have been lost in translation.

II   *The Style*

The style of *The Salt of the Earth* remains its most striking feature for the native reader. Thus the "microanalysis" of Wittlin's text presents difficulties when based on a translation, for we cannot discuss sentence structure, rhythm and all the other sound effects which play a major role in the book. The varying length of sentences and clauses, the smooth and graceful placement of words (Polish unlike English, has no compulsory word order), his so-called inversions and repetitions (especially triple ones)—all this has a rhythmical impact on the native reader who is captivated by this particular kind of prose almost as much as he is by the hexameters of Wittlin's *Odyssey*. One could point to the use of leitmotifs; one could even speak of certain recurring rhythmical units of a kind usually considered the prerogative of poetry. Wittlin's prose is permeated with alliterations, assonances, anaphoras and other rhythmic and melodic effects. Leitmotifs frequently serve as links in the chain of continuity (The leitmotif of "waiting for the war's end" is repeated in several chapters). Sometimes they stress a thought of special concern to the author, or serve to reinforce the emotional impact of a phrase or image.

Wittlin composed for the eye as well as for the ear; he tries to eternalize the living word, to strike the right tone in every sentence. This rhythmical organization of language helps the author to harmonize such diverse elements as archaisms, neologisms, dialect words and phrases, and to bring his prose close to poetry. So, too, does his highly poetic concentration, where almost every sentence has its point and the similes and metaphors extend and reverberate as they should in any good epic and poetic work.

As we have already learned in the previous chapter the punch line is often ironic. Irony linked with parody and the grotesque seems to predominate in the book, for all its strong lyrical strain. One could almost say that *The Salt of the Earth* belongs in the realm of ironic literature or at least sometimes closely approximates it. This becomes all the more evident when one considers the concept of the book as a whole, as one meditates on Peter Niewiadomski, "irony's substitute for the hero"[7]—and the fate that has him perish in an Italian uniform and be selected as . . . the Italian Unknown Soldier in Rome![8] An ironical intent is clear in the title of Part I of the Trilogy—the Evangelical "salt of the earth" which has lost its savor, in the paradoxical title of Part II—"A Healthy Death" and in the somewhat incongruous title of Part III—"A Hole in the Sky." Irony seems to color both the author's vision and his relationship to the world. However, one must point out that it is a positive irony in Solger's sense,[9] the irony that presupposes truth. Armed with irony, Wittlin sets out to demolish all false fronts, to strip the war and the war lords once and for all of false glory and pretense. It is Peter's function to be the filter through which truth is separated from lies. His refreshing reactions defamiliarize the usual and the stereotyped. This "defamiliarization," coupled with irony is not infrequently used by Wittlin for satirical purposes. Irony is not always satire. It must be qualified for there are as many kinds of irony as there are authors using it and objects evoking it. To illustrate this point we could single out many passages from *The Salt of the Earth* expressing every conceivable shade of irony. For instance there is the description of the "parade march" in Chapter 8, or the magnificent scene of the recruiting of the poor conscripts by the Military Board in Chapter 3 in which both defamiliarization and irony contribute to form a satirical edge. Northrop Frye says that "a militant irony is satire."[10] Wittlin's "militant" irony is directed at the mighty of this earth, at Franz Josef and his aides (the Emperor is often compared to God and Zeus), at all those who exercise their power at other people's expense, even sending men to their death. We have already indicated the important parodistic parallel between the Christian Church and Christian morality and the "militant church" of the "brethren in the Emperor Franz Josef" (p. 89). This parallel is sustained throughout the book by images and words and the ironical application of Biblical quotations and references to the new "Church." Service Regulations I and II are referred to mockingly as the Old and the New Testaments. In the Declaration of War Franz Josef complains in "liturgical and pathetic phrases of the wicked and infamous Serbs" (p. 51). The Austrian Emperor is "all-powerful," he summons "both the living and the dead" (p. 55). He gives the Galician fugitives of the Jewish faith a new "Promised Land in Moravia . . ." (p. 120). He is invisible: "The Emperor is in the air, invisible like God, Whom also no man can see with his eyes" (p. 105). The Emperor re-creates the soldiers, who are to fight and to fall for him, by giving them a uniform: "And as God created man in His likeness, so the Emperor presented men with a uniform, to give them some sort of likeness to himself" (pp. 295-96). The religious vocabulary and imagery are most consistently used by Wittlin for ironic and parodistic purposes in Chapters 9 and 10, which are devoted to Bachmatiuk, the counterfeit creator of the new breed of men. Words and phrases like *faith, meditation, devotion, chaplain, nun, priest, cell, missionary, the holy spirit of duty* (p. 265), *neophytes* (p. 274) and many others from the same semantic field are common in this part of the book.

The extent of this irony becomes still more noticeable when one takes account of the abundance of contrasts—both explicit and implicit—and their function. The juxtaposition of opposites—of good and evil, God and the Devil, heaven and earth, the word and the flesh, the truth and lies, body and soul, war and peace, life and death, the military and civilian worlds, the human and the inhuman, faith and fear, friends and foes, just and unjust, loyalty and treason, love and hate, new and old, right and left give the author countless opportunities to employ all the multiple shades of irony, thus investing the book with hidden dynamics which replace any that the plot could supply.

A reversal of values, itself an important ironic and satirical device also characterizes the war much better than could any direct description. Thus night becomes day (Chapter 6), because the army ignores the motions of the celestial bodies; health becomes a drawback in the face of the Draft Board; an airplane appears in place of the dove of peace following the solar eclipse, also described in Chapter 6. The first enemy of "our folk" in the camp of Andrasfalva is paradoxically their own corporal.

An example of an implicit juxtaposition yielding a deeply ironic effect can be found in two adjacent passages: one concerns Ukrainian peasants who give information to the enemy, the other is about the Galician governor-general who piles up "written evidence of the love, the loyalty, and attachment felt by the *whole* population of the Crownlands towards His Majesty" (p. 113; italics mine, Z. Y.) The written evidence is not to be trusted, as all written and printed words must be suspected of originating with the Devil, against whom Wittlin wages his private war.[11] The following sentence gives the whole scene a comic twist: "So multitudinous was the evidence that it piled up in a great mound around the Throne, and it was all His Majesty could do to make his way to the Imperial study" (p. 113).

As we can see, Wittlin's irony reaches deep and wide, drawing into its net people and events of the most diverse nature to subject them to the author's judgment. Ironic ambiguities, as we have noted earlier, might also point toward the future, a revival of the old device of premonition. Thus, describing the time-table of the Imperial and Royal State Railways which ceased to be valid with the outbreak of the war, the author comments: "The official time-table hung there useless, and inconsequent as a printed funeral notice left hanging outside a house which has buried its dead *yesterday*" (p. 49; italics mine, Z. Y.). The Polish original has an important epithet, "old," qualifying the funeral notices, which helps to disclose the meaning alluded to in the paragraph on the same page which reads: "The *new* posters (Declaration of War, Z. Y.) had been drying for an hour on the waiting-room wall. They were large and white, and serious-looking, with no pictures, no smiling waiters or sphinx-like women. Their freshness was provocative" (p. 49). It could be that this juxtaposing of "old" and "new" has the following meaning: the *new* posters are like *new* funeral notices announcing the dead who will be buried *tomorrow*. . . . (Italics mine, Z. Y.)

Irony also often underlies Wittlin's witticisms, his most apt epigrams and aphorisms. Here, for example, are some of Peter's reflections on how he might be freed from his oath: "Promotion to corporal, or death for the Emperor? Maybe neither would serve. Peter could never hope to be a corporal; corporals must read and write. But he could easily become a corpse; there was no schooling needed for that" (p. 182). One should stress that a promotion to corporal as a means to be freed from the oath is in itself an ironic incongruity, which serves to introduce a quip.

Wittlin has the insight to perceive clearly the duality and contradiction in all things and it is this insight that is the source of all these devices usually designated as "comic" which include both humorous and ironic devices. Wittlin delights in spotting and presenting us with paradoxical situations, paradox being the heart of irony. In Wittlin's work irony embraces not only derision, scorn, and sarcasm but also a benevolent, humane smile at human weakness. While he reserves his most crushing irony for the "powerful ones" of this world, those who are supposed to be "the salt of the earth," he smiles at the "meek in heart," who themselves lack the faculty of irony: Peter and the other inhabitants of Topory-Czernielica. Wittlin smiles at them as one smiles at children. This kind of irony is expressed mostly by means of a Biblical stylization which makes their "deeds" and "sins" humorous. It is also achieved through an ironic retelling of their own stories, tales and gossip which enlivens and diversifies the author's narrative technique.

Wittlin is interested not merely in the comic as opposed to the tragic, but in tragicomic elements and effects; according to him these are best suited for reproducing the myth of the contemporary world.[12] Elements of the grotesque are quite evident in the Prologue in the portrayal of Franz Josef and his aides, in the comparison of the terrible "recruit-eater" Bachmatiuk to a "nun," a "vestal virgin" and a "chaplain"—all in one breath! They are also prominent in the superb description of the bribe-taking Dr. Jellinek with his real and metaphorical spurs. "He refused to be parted from his spurs. He wore them from early morning till late at night. He would have liked, had it been possible, to buckle them to his bedroom slippers, or to his naked feet. . . .

The jingle of his spurs called up for him, at times, visions of glorious knights, proud knights. . . . Mounted on a dream horse and brandishing a sword, he leaped all the barriers which life had ranged in front of him because he was a Jew" (p. 87). The whole of Chapter 3 describing the mock Last Judgement has grotesque elements which heighten the tragicomic effect.

The tragic aspect of human life where death lies in wait everywhere is not usually stated explicitly. The impending doom of the little station and the imminent destruction of the entire way of life of an enormous Empire is mirrored more convincingly in a "hidden-way" of presentation: in the large number of metaphors and similes which I would like to call, not at all facetiously, "morbid metaphors" and "sinister similes." Applied to both people and things they are inevitably connected with death, murder, destruction. These metaphors and similes already appear in the Prologue where "Berchtold's cloying perfume floated like incense over the bodies of the murdered dead" (p. 15). They continue in Chapter 1 where a wastebasket is compared to a grave of murdered (not "fallen" as in the English translation) soldiers, and where the station's ticket window is closed like "the mouth of the dead" (p. 48). In Chapter 2 the voice of the gendarme reads the mobilization order like "an actor who reads a death sentence" (p. 62) and the blue mobilization paper lies "in Peter's motionless hands, like a pictured saint clasped between the stiff fingers of the dead" (p. 66). From Chapter 3 on their number increases to such an extent that it is impossible to cite all of them here: a scale for measuring one's height reminds Peter of a gallows; the draftees' clothes look like hanged men; Peter compares himself to a "slaughtered animal." Later, in Chapter 4, the Red Cross cars are compared to graves and the same comparison is applied to the barracks in the camp at Andrasfalva. Even the station signboard (Chapter 5) is "like a dead body." The oath to the Emperor is likened to "extreme unction administered to the dying"; the suitcase Peter takes with him for the journey to Hungary is compared to a child's coffin (Chapter 6). The darkness which envelops Topory-Czernielica during the eclipse of the sun is referred to as the "pall of darkness." Chapter 8 is especially full of morbid similes and metaphors. Wittlin used the "moribund" images consistently throughout the book to create the atmosphere of impending doom which makes *The Salt of the Earth* so fascinating for the contemporary reader.

There is another group of metaphors which deserves to be singled out—those having to do with war, mobilization and the imminent destruction of the old way of life. One thinks of the complex of "war metaphors" and similes which replaces the complex of "agricultural metaphors" and similes, so suitable to the rustic background of Topory-Czernielica, as soon as the mobilization takes effect. The war not only carries off the best men of the village "as though a flail had thrashed the best grain from the stalk" (p. 123), but also takes over the earth with everything thereon and even the sky. . . . Soldiers are compared to sheaves of grain, and sheaves to soldiers (p. 138) in the best epic tradition. Even pots on the fence look like "helmets of the crusaders" (p. 139). The mention of the mobilization of the storks and a "storming party of geese" complete this picture in Chapter 7, when Peter is heading for the Army. Wittlin even describes a battle in the sky, repeating an image from his "Lullaby for My Baby Daughter." It is interesting to observe the switch from agricultural imagery to imagery of a military sort in process, so to speak: If the falling stars are likened to a *herd* in Chapter 5, the clouds in Chapter 8 are likened to "*detachments* of sheep" which are pursued by a sun—the "fiery dog"—another classical reminiscence. Elsewhere mattresses are likened to shields (So is the sun, for that matter!)—a reminder of the "Homeric" technique in which Wittlin was trained. In the Prologue "armies of buttons, whistles, belts" closely parallel the armies of soldiers. Later a retreating army is compared to an army of "extinguished lanterns." The war has a levelling, almost surrealistic effect upon everything it touches.[13] There is in general little difference in the way people and things are described in the book. Wittlin's world, a new reality he creates by likening his people to things and things to people, somewhat resembles the weird world of Gogol, a writer with whom he feels a spiritual affinity. Wittlin has an extraordinary ability to see life in everything—a wooden plank in which he senses "an eternal life," expressing itself in tears of tar (!), animals like Peter's dog Bass endowed with a marked personality; the personified rivers Czeremosz and Pruth—(also reminiscent of Gogol) which are ready to come and bid the enlisted men farewell. Examples are too numerous to be listed here, but, as we have already noted (see Chapter I) anthropomorphization is one of the author's favorite devices. Again, this is not without Homer's influence; moreover it is well suited to Peter's primitive mentality, to whom Jung's dictum on the primitive world in which "everything has psychic qualities"[14] could well be applied. It seems to me that this talent for making everything come alive accounts, to a great extent, for the indelible effect produced by the book, even in translation. This talent enables Wittlin to create a host of interrelated metaphors and similes which extend into the realm of myth; thus a haystack becomes a giant wearing a cap; the station's crane merges with Peter, the porter, and Peter represents metonymically not only all the Huculs in the book but also all the soldiers known and unknown. This is probably what Thomas Mann had in mind when he wrote that in Wittlin's book the typical extends into the sphere of the mythical.[15]

We have already mentioned the personification of war to the degree that it actually becomes a *dramatis persona* of the book. War which comes over to the embankment in black boots and confronts Peter . . . is a metonymy: it is not the war as such who comes but merely an official carrying the summons to war. But Wittlin's hand creates a new mythical figure not unlike a new god of war, or the messenger of a Greek god, who is geared with mocking irony by the author to the contemporary scene, revealing its bureaucratic and unpoetic nature as soon as he opens his mouth . . . with a golden tooth. Even before the war spreads metonymically, assuming different forms, the station master, who learns of its outbreak from the telegraph, disentangles himself from "coils of paper covered with Morse Code" and shakes "the war from his feet" (p. 48). Niewiadomski, holding a new poster announcing the war, is "holding the war in his hand. This war in his hand was not yet unfurled. It was shut tight like new buds in spring" (p. 47). This grotesque simile together with the metonymy underscore the sinister import of the phrase.

We see that Wittlin uses both metaphor and metonymy with equal effectiveness. He is especially good at substituting a state of mind or emotion for the people who are in its grip, thus creating from such an abstraction a separate entity imbued with ephemeral life. Terror, Fear, Aggression, Revolt, Treason, Language—all these live, move, act as if quite separate from those whom they characterize. Unfortunately such effects are more often than not lost in the English translation. Thus, when in Chapter 6 of the Polish original we read that "Fear was to travel together with the last classes of *Landsturm* to Hungary" the translator omits this, substituting a "smoother" phrase: "But fear still crouched deep in their hearts, for today they were to entrain for Hungary" (p. 163). Similarly, when Wittlin says of a foreign language that it "lives enjoying only the rights of a subtenant" in a Ukrainian village the translator renders this simply as a "foreign talk" which "was expected to keep humbly in the background" (p. 190). The translator seems to have been over-wary of Wittlin's bold way of using metonymy to achieve an almost cubist effect as, for example, in his description of the soldiers' parade: "*Sleeves flung themselves* rhythmically to the left, to the right, to the left, to the right, as though moving invisible meadows" (p. 214; italics mine, Z. Y.). The translator has this as: "The arms swung in unison to the left, to the right, as though moving invisible meadows" (p. 214). Such metonymic devices of substituting bodies, parts of bodies or even parts of clothing for their owners can render description very expressive; for example: "Hairy buttocks, like those of monkeys, and formless masses of flesh swayed on their chairs near whiteskinned figures as slim and supple as any girl's" (p. 77). Metonymy can be a valuable device for conveying some powerful emotion, or expression; weeping for instance. Wittlin writes in the Prologue that "the railway stations in Vienna and Budapest and Prague began to weep"—an obvious transfer of people's emotions to their surroundings. Again the translator is more "realistic" and writes that "the railway stations . . . are filled with the sound of weeping . . ." (p. 27). In Chapter 6, however, Wittlin's metonymy comes through in translation as well. A scream from two old Jewish women evokes the weeping of the whole crowd of villagers who are gathered to see their men off to war: "The whole station caught fire at the Jewish flames and suddenly shook with sobs" (p. 173).

In his role as a poet, however, Wittlin seems to be attracted more by metaphor, perhaps because it gives him an opportunity to exploit the multivocality and ambiguity of words, as is more often the case in poetry than in "straight" prose. The same ambiguity is at the root of puns which are quite frequent in *The*

Salt of the Earth. Some of these were reproduced in translation, but others were not. For instance: "To say that he carried burdens epitomized Peter's life. Even in childhood he carried within him seeds of that malady which it is the fashion to attribute to the French . . ." (p. 35). And then: "In addition it was Peter's lot to *carry* (italics mine, Z. Y.) on his back the weight of his father's sheepskin coat and also to *bear* his name" (p. 35). "Bear" can be a substitute for "carry" here, since it has both meanings, as in Polish. Another pun came through very well in English: "For the moment Peter was ready to *break* his oath. But what could he do? Was he to jump the train? And perhaps to *break* an arm or leg . . ." (p. 185; italics mine).

Another favorite device of Wittlin should be mentioned. It is the device of the so-called "realized metaphor" called also "literalization," i. e., the replacing of the figurative meaning of something with its literal meaning. This, incorporated into the text, helps to stretch out the narrative (not Wittlin's forte), and is also used for comic effects. Here are some examples: "Peter himself was the fruit of a lawful *marriage bed*. The *bed* in question was still standing in a hut, now much decayed, at the far end of the village of Topory" (p. 36). "The Emperor had not forgotten Peter Niewiadomski; he had reserved him for the *dark hour*. And now *the hour* had come. Not dark, but light . . ." (p. 56; italics mine, Z. Y.). This device is especially suitable as a mirror of Peter's naive consciousness. "What was it that one was not to sow? Panic? What was panic? Some obnoxious seed perhaps, or some plant like tobacco. Stern punishment awaited those who secretly planted tobacco. Peter sowed nothing and raised nothing, except beans and cabbages and sunflowers" (pp. 126-27).

Irony, parody, the grotesque, puns, as we find them in *The Salt of the Earth* would often be out of place in an old-fashioned epic, but they help to make this book a new kind of epic, an epic of the twentieth century. Irony here reveals that what was dressing itself up in the garb of a new myth of the twentieth century and was unworthy of the name. Wittlin destroyed the myths of the mighty Emperor and of the "unknown soldier" as these have been officially propagated. In creating his saga of the patient foot-soldier he erected a fine monument to one of the sons of the "Hucul earth" and all the other "sons" for whom Peter stands. *The Salt of the Earth is* a finished work of art in which the whole structure and the compositional unity encompasses everything down to the minutest detail, in which all dissonances are resolved into harmony. Nothing is lost, nothing is too small for an author who knows how to achieve unity by manipulating microscopic particles into a whole. The coming of doom is evoked by means of "moribund" metaphors which point to the philosophy of the work, and not by the novelist's direct statements. In *The Salt of the Earth* the author knows how to preserve the "fiction" of a novel, even what appears to be a historical novel, by presenting events in chronological order and using many authentic details. But what the modern reader most values are some of the "moments" described; for example that of the signing of the Declaration of War in the Prologue, which seems to last forever and thereby to have become indelible. The reader will never forget the little station of Topory-Czernielica, a microcosm lovingly created by an artist who knew how to reproduce its soul, which grows in dimensions to represent the soul of the whole Austro-Hungarian Empire and perhaps even of the whole world.

CHAPTER 6

Orpheus in the Inferno of the Twentieth Century

I An Unintentional Autobiography

ORPHEUS in the Inferno of the Twentieth Century (*Orfeusz w piekle XX wieku*) is a book of Wittlin's essays and other prose writings, spanning a forty-year period. It was published in Paris (in 1963) by the library of *Kultura* as Volume I of a projected multi-volume edition of his works designed to commemorate forty years of the writer's creative achievement. Volume II of the works, consisting mainly of poetry, is now in preparation. In addition to the articles, speeches, addresses and book reviews of various dates *Orpheus* includes three books which were published separately earlier in Wittlin's career: *War, Peace and a Poet's Soul (Wojna, pokoj i dusza poety)* (1925), a book of post-World War I essays—here incomplete; *Stages (Etapy)* (1932), a travelogue complete; and *My Lwów (Mój Lwów)* (1946), a book of memoirs, complete. *Orpheus* is divided into four parts. Part I consists of selected articles from the book *War, Peace and a Poet's Soul*—which were written in the first decade after World War I—and is rounded out by the articles on topical subjects written during and after World War II. Part II consists of travel sketches (the bulk of it comes from the *Stages*) supplemented by more recent travel impressions and the author's first glimpses of the U.S.A. Part III is made up of *My Lwów*, which is a colorful account of the author's favorite city plus a few other reminiscences in which the author's past and present are artfully and naturally intermingled and fused into one highly satisfying and esthetic whole. Part IV is devoted mostly to literary and theatrical criticism, to Wittlin's reactions to the relevant cultural topics of the time. It contains some important assessments of his contemporaries in different countries, both dead and living. There is a predominance of necrologies—an imbalance which is not surprising, in view of the high importance and positive value Wittlin attaches to death and all its manifestations.

In his Preface Wittlin refers to the book as an unintentional autobiography, a self-portrait without any touching up, since—in contrast to his usual tendency to perfectionism—his early essays are here reproduced unchanged in order to give a genuine picture of the author as he was when he wrote them. In fact, the book could be considered material for an inner autobiography (what Wittlin called elsewhere an "ideological" autobiography) which contains traits of his inner character and at the same time reflects the whole epoch through the reactions of a highly sensitive, sophisticated, honest and talented writer.

It is fascinating to watch Wittlin's countenance change in different geographical, historical and cultural climates, to see his spiritual metamorphosis as the time passes. It would be virtually impossible, though, to reproduce these changes for the American reader (up to now, only a few essays are available in English translation) if only because one must bear in mind that *Orpheus* not only gives an account of the forty years of the author's highly active and thoughtful life, but also embraces many centuries of our Judeo-Christian civilization, beginning with classical antiquity, continuing through the Middle Ages, the Renaissance, the eighteenth and nineteenth centuries and ending with the literary currents of our own day. Wittlin displays a broad and often also deep knowledge and learning in all these phases of mankind's spiritual development.

His geographical range includes all the major European countries: France (his second homeland), Italy, Germany, Austria, Yugoslavia and also the United States seen with the fresh eye of an exceptionally perceptive and seasoned traveler who is endowed with the ability to search out and to discover the innermost essence, the hidden nerve of every phenomenon which he scrutinizes.

One suspects that Wittlin was eager to preserve all the varied background material for posterity so that his own image would remain faithful and not become a distorted mask of a "person without a background"—an expression found in another volume of memoirs by Wittlin's contemporary and compatriot, the late Waclaw Lednicki. Wittlin asserts in the Preface that he has

decided to issue his unplanned autobiography primarily because
of its historical background: prewar times, the war years 1914-
1918-1920, the interbellum period (1919-1939), a great deal of
refugee traveling and now exile, permanent, it seems, in the
United States.

II *In the Name of Sincerity . . .*

Orpheus is almost boundlessly rich in content and is still
further enriched by the author's complete honesty and total lack
of any kind of smugness and self-complacency. He follows in
this, as in many other respects, his theoretical pronouncements
on autobiography which we find in the Preface, in his articles on
"St. Augustine and the Theater" and in "Pasternak's Attempt at
Autobiography" (all in *Orpheus*). Here we may illustrate Wittlin's outlook for American readers with some brief quotations,
since all these essays have so far appeared only in Polish. Says
Wittlin, "Even the most sincere autobiographies are composed
with the intention that they will be autobiographies. . . . And
every composition—even that which seems chaotic—must obey
the laws of harmony and counterpoint" (p. 8). "There are autobiographies in which the author clearly suggests that the reader
should look at him as the author sees fit." Those autobiographies
whose authors desire only to realize in full who they are, in
what kind of world they are living and to what end—are of
more value.

"It often happens, however, that the author of an autobiography aims at fascinating the reader with the repulsive traits
of his own character. The autobiographer or memoir writer who
is free from the desire to be liked or disliked is a rare species"
(p. 8). But even someone who is capable of a lofty indifference
to his own person, still will construct a "panoramic," artificial
tableau of his own life. Nor does the person of the autobiographer
always determine the value of an autobiography (p. 611). For
example, we will never believe a statesman who is trying to
convince us of his virtue and truthfulness simply because "he
himself has said it." "Nobody can at the same time be his own
divinity and his own apostle," concludes Wittlin aphoristically
(p. 611). He adds sarcastically that today there is a plethora of
autobiographical works of a sort which convey a distinct impression that their authors consider the mere fact of their exist-

ence a quite sufficient motive for writing about themselves. At best, if they are sincere, they give us documents of pride or self-love. Wittlin discusses sincerity in *Orpheus* in an essay on "St. Augustine and the Theatre" (1930) which contains very interesting reflections on that quality. There is, he says, sincerity in front of other people which yields "masterpieces of observation, judgment and irony" (p. 392); sincerity with oneself, without concern for other people, "confessing oneself not in the smooth language of one's listeners, but in a tangled, stammering language of one's soul; sincerity before God, "as it were a constant, life-long confession in *articulo mortis* . . . This highest kind of sincerity is accessible only to saints and martyrs" (p. 392). Wittlin finds the synthesis of all the three kinds of sincerity in the *Confessions of St. Augustine* and is full of admiration for their author who "with the same simplicity confides in God, in himself and in us" (p. 392).

Wittlin himself in *Orpheus* makes many a confession "in the name of sincerity which my pen has professed since the time it was first granted me to hold it" (p. 117). And while Wittlin stresses the mutability of his unintentional self-portrait, we would like to stress its constant, recurring features whose stability assures us of their importance in the author's spiritual make-up. Sincerity, loyalty to Truth and an effort to write *"in articulo mortis"* (cf. essay on "Posthumous Works," which we shall refer to later) have made Wittlin wage war against every form of hypocrisy and idle talk, against every type of falsehood whether in books or in people, in whole nations or governments or in one's own memory which Wittlin twice calls a "falsifier" (pp. 325 and 360). The highest Truth, the Ultimate Truth, is for Wittlin God's Truth—Truth being the highest value in Wittlin's Christian hierarchy of values. There is hardly an essay in the whole of *Orpheus* in which Wittlin's devotion and dedication to Truth, his constant striving after it and concern with it does not come to the fore in one way or another. In his early essays, Wittlin saw the poet's truth as touching upon the sphere of God's truth (see, for instance, the brilliant essay on the tragic theater "Empty Theatre," p. 388). In another early article (from the book *War, Peace and the Poet's Soul*) entitled "The Last Resort" (1931), Wittlin proposed that writers should return to the old tradition of Lord Byron and Adam Mickiewicz, and "convert every word into

an instrument of *truth* (Italics mine, Z. Y.) for which we would
be ready to give our lives." This Romantic and Expressionistic
tradition is also reflected in Wittlin's belief that the writer's
word is "a word of honor" (p. 131), "no matter whether it is
given on paper, in life, or in the face of death." He praises those
writers who love the truth and never betray it, "who use the
language exclusively for telling the truth" (p. 488) and whose
life and work present us with models of harmony between what
they are and what they write and preach about. (Cf. "Strug's
Lesson"—"Lekcja Struga.") He praises another writer's power to
"unveil the romantic grandeur of a part of Warsaw, a power im-
parted by the *love of truth* (p. 483) (Italics mine, Z. Y.). He
admires and praises Pope Pius XI for his defense of truth (in
1938, in a letter from Castel Gandolfo, in which Pius XI offered
his life for the sake of peace in the world). At one point Wittlin
offers the profound observation that "during those periods when
human souls starve of hunger for Truth, only faith can save
them from starvation" (p. 109). But he observes elsewhere that
God sends us the necessary courage in the fight for truth (p. 493).
Wittlin has such courage. He voices his convictions and his profound belief in Truth and Righteousness unhesitatingly and without concern over their acceptance or rejection. Thus, in an illuminating essay "On the Need for a New Morality" ("O potrzebie
nowej moralnosci") he expounds truth as the only truly useful
value for a postwar moral rehabilitation of Poland and holds it
up as an objective for émigré writers. His everpresent concern
for truth comes out even in the guise of wit, as when he remarks
in one essay (p. 585): "That sort of people known as Poles are
among the most fearless in the world; indeed they fear nothing
except calling the truth by its own name" and adds, this time in
earnest: "But is it not just this which is the vocation and historical
mission of a writer?" (p. 590). In the same article he says that
émigré writers enjoy limitless freedom of thought and expression,
a freedom which would have been equally impossible in pre-Sep-
tember Poland and in postwar Poland, and which affords the
Polish émigré writer an opportunity to drink to the bottom from
the bitter cup of *truth* (Italics mine, Z. Y.) without regard as to
whether it is becoming to us or not (p. 590). Wittlin praises
highly American literature for intellectual honesty in the Preface
to Hersey's *Hiroshima* (p. 137). He singles out such modern

French writers as George Bernanos, Julian Green, Emanuel Bove, Marcel Arland, Jean Cocteau and certain others for subjecting their readers to virtual torture "in order to force truth from this decitful world" (p. 195). He wishes that young Polish writers might learn truthfulness from their French colleagues. And he confesses that while living in Poland he himself often experienced the need to transfer his spirit to St. Honorine in Normandy (cf. his book *Stages*) in order to "transform the everyday Polish word into the word of my inner honor, of my truth!" (p. 204). This brings us to another concept which Wittlin rates very highly in his hierarchy of values and which is, as we shall see, directly connected with the Truth:—the Word. We have already mentioned an essay in which the poet's truth is assigned a place next to God's truth, since a real poet when he loves truth creates his own world in his words. To Wittlin an example of an ideal poet is Rainer Maria Rilke, a Christian who corresponds to his youthful idea of the Romantic poet as a being of a higher order. (Cf. his beautiful essay, "R. M. Rilke and his Stundenbuch" ("R. M. Rilke i jego 'Ksiega godzin.'") Wittlin has never wavered in his belief in Truth and that the poet's art is destined to seek out this truth and reveal it to others. In an early essay, already cited, we find the following words: "True creators will never offer us a counterfeit wine and bread" (p. 386). Wittlin calls the poetic truth "all important" and "unshakable" (p. 503), and superior to the historical truth, because "an honest fiction, an invention is also truth" (p. 468). He quotes the German writer Alfred Döblin, whom he knew personally, to the effect that "a poet never errs, so long as he remains true to his vision." Wittlin regards the "law of transfiguration" as the highest law for an artist (p. 517). (See his illuminating essay devoted to Thomas Mann, which has appeared elsewhere in English.)[1]

In his youth Wittlin cherished a belief that the word and poetry could change the world and that the poets who during the First World War were trying to save "the remnants of human conscience" (p. 35) and not the priests, who had kept silent, should pray for peace. This utopian hope in the miraculous power of the poet's word was renounced by Wittlin a few years later when in an essay "From the Recollections of an Ex-Pacifist" ("Ze wspomnien bylego pacyfisty") he stated that "one should live within the limitations imposed by fate which are not going to be changed by our books, even the most beautiful ones" (p. 84). We have observed a similar change in Wittlin's poetry.

However, during World War II, in the Epilogue to an important book he edited together with Manfred Kridl and Wladyslaw Malinowski, *For Your Freedom and Ours,*[2] he reminded "lovers of action instead of words" of the first verse in the Gospel of St. John: "In the beginning was the Word . . ." and added: "And if what is happening now is the end, the end of the old world, then there will be a word at the end and a word will renew the world, it will rescue or annihilate. The word breeds love or sows hate. Cannons, tanks, and devastation were born of words. Let us trust that out of words a new life will be born."[3] In an article "Empty Words" ("Puste slowa") written during the war in which he appeals for the rehabilitation of words which have lost their true meaning because of prolonged use and misuse, he speaks of his words as his weapon, and in another article written about the same time he says that writers must defend their language against destruction (p. 120) and that they constitute a kind of defensive fire which is nearer to the heaven than even barrage balloons (p. 120). Thus, in a time of crisis his belief in the word and its power acquired new momentum. But later still, sadly, he came to the conclusion that "no word in any human language is an instrument of perfect sincerity" (p. 629). If, back in 1932, in St. Honorine des Pertes in Normandy, he was able to communicate with his "soul" (a word he now puts in quotation marks, cf. The Preface) thirty years later, in New York he has discovered that "we do not think for ourselves by means of words. Our thought in its pure state uses other, still undetermined, instruments. Only when we want to convey our thoughts to others do we fall back upon words" *(Ibid.).* However, "the more easily comprehensible are such words, especially in poetry, the more they lose their virgin purity . . . A writer cannot dispense with language, with words. The best he can do is *deform them* (Italics mine, Z. Y.) for the sake of sincerity and purity" (p. 629).

III   *The Posthumous Works*

The essay from which the above quotation comes is one of the most fascinating in the whole book. It is here that Wittlin advocates writing *"in articulo mortis,"* another notion to which he has consistently remained faithful. The essay is called "Posthumous Works," and the title is set in large type. Wittlin tells us how, while still a young writer, he decided not to publish anything at all during his lifetime and instead to write only for posterity. He would be thus enabled to escape both the rules and the anarchy of the literary marketplace where products of the human mind and imagination are priced and sold and the status of the writer is evaluated and reevaluated. He need not fear the "rat race" of the publishing business and could disregard the so-called "social demand" of his time. Since he would know nothing of his future readers and would be unconcerned with their wants and needs he could strive, unhampered, to achieve absolute perfection in his work. By "posthumous works" Wittlin means not only those published after a writer's death, but also works written in the presence of death by writers who were so much attracted by death that it became their constant companion, men like Kafka, Hemingway or Jan Lechon, who created "under its auspices." It was as if this intense awareness of death had opened up for them a truer knowledge of life. If a writer writes "in articulo mortis" everything he has to say may acquire the special weight and importance of eternal farewell. "The proximity of death may make his song more intense and noble, filling it with transcendental tension and radiation" (p. 636).

Wittlin did not actually stop publishing—for writing was his profession—but his conception of "posthumous works" made him extremely hesitant and careful in shaping and wording his opinions. It was as if these opinions, sentences and images "were going to live independently of my own destiny or relations with other people, as if after the completion of my work my life was simply to vanish" (p. 637). This is an important confession on Wittlin's part. It may serve to explain his constant striving for artistic perfection, his rewriting of the *Hymns*, his retranslating of the *Odyssey*, his laborious reworking of the second part of the trilogy *Salt of the Earth* which became such a long and drawn out process. Moreover, this tendency is closely related also to Wittlin's lifelong intimacy with death—a theme which we have been observing throughout this book. His loyalty to Death is no less than his fidelity to the Truth and the Word. It is significant that Orpheus, whose name gives the title to this book is a connecting link between life and death. While we may in part accept

Wittlin's explanation of how the book acquired this title, we also
cannot overlook Wittlin's fidelity to the Orphic viewpoint of in-
teraction of life and death. Even if the essay "Orpheus in the
Inferno of the Twentieth Century" originated on the occasion
of a concert given by a well-known Polish tenor Jan Kiepura,
what Wittlin has to say here about Orpheus is much more important than his remarks about the actual concert. It is characteristic of Wittlin that an unimportant event, a trivial detail,
often stimulates him to deep reflections and conclusions. This
is especially evident in the *Stages* (Part II of *Orpheus* and also
in its other sections). In the above-mentioned essay Wittlin compares the mythical Orpheus, half-God and half-poet, to the poets
of the contemporary world, observing sadly that while the mythical Orpheus was mighty and knew how to tame wild beasts, the
poets of today have not even the power to tame the wild beast
that is shut within the human heart. "Nobody's song," says Wittlin "has stopped volcanoes of hate from erupting, or prevented
bombs from setting on fire whole cities during the last war.
While for the mythical Orpheus hell was located underground,
the hell of modern Orpheuses is here on earth and is inhabited
by living people. . . ." However, art may still often help "to conquer fear, to conquer death and to conquer time which leads us
on inevitably toward death. . . . Thanks to poetry and music,
both of which Orpheus symbolizes, we "who are imprisoned in
space, are able to rest in time" (p. 383). But even more important
is what Wittlin says of Orpheus in the Preface to this volume:
"Everything songful within us originates, at least in part, in
Orpheus and his tragic combat with death" (p. 15). A poet
must fight against death and must attempt to ring from hell
its mysteries. Nor should the vision of death ever leave the
poet. (Wittlin says this in praise of Rilke, one of his "eternal
companions," p. 463, but we are justified in applying it to poets
in general and to Wittlin himself in particular, on the basis of
evidence scattered throughout the entire book.) Wittlin's voyages
in space and time which encompass all Europe and the United
States and our entire cultural heritage seem to us to have very
often the one and the same objective: the conquest of Death
while one always remains aware of its actuality. It is this faculty
that enables Wittlin's gaze to pierce unerringly and like an X-ray
through the transient surface of any phenomenon to its essential

and eternal core. This rare quality is apparent in all parts of the book, but especially in Part II *(Stages)* and Part IV, where his very unusual necrologies and essay-type book reviews reveal his aim: not only to bring the vision of Death nearer to us, but to try at the same time to conquer it! Every observant reader of the book can see clearly that Wittlin converses with the dead as much as he does with the living and perhaps even more vigorously and exhaustingly. On sleepless nights or in broad daylight he is visited by the dead comrades of his youth who "jump suddenly out of darkened gates and arise from the empty benches in city parks . . ." (p. 434). "Perhaps those who die young continue living in each of us and will perish finally only with the death of their last contemporary?" asks Wittlin. "But who knows," he continues "perhaps it is the other way around—a certain part of us dies along with them?" (p. 434). Thus echoes mean more to Wittlin than the original sounds despite his sensitivity to sounds as such. His Lwow is ultimately, as we shall see, a city of shadows where the footsteps of those who are no longer alive· resound to Wittlin with horrible clarity. Thus, too, Wittlin believes that in Paris, in Monmartre, he hears the footsteps of his great compatriot Mickiewicz, who lived in exile there. Links between living and dying, frontiers between life and death, good and evil, body and soul (p. 244) Wittlin calls "problems of the Borderland." In the brilliant essay "The Death of Tuwim" (p. 599) he avows that all these problems hold a magnetic attraction to him. This is why he values Tuwim so highly—Tuwim who was a "poet of the Borderland" and was at home "on the border between the world and eternity" (Tuwim's phrase). Tuwim was a poet "by God's grace" and his poetry is for Wittlin an argument for the existence of God. On one occasion he offered this argument more or less as a joke having in mind the discrepancy between Tuwim's greatness as a poet and certain human, all too human traits which he displayed as a man. But after Tuwim's death he reasserted it seriously in a beautiful tribute to one of the great poets of the twentieth century. No less revealing of Wittlin's relation to Death is another tribute to a tragically deceased friend, a Polish poet of the *Skamander* group, Jan Lechon (Leszek Serafinowicz: 1899-1956), who leaped to his death from a New York skyscraper. Wittlin, who elsewhere in his book prays —in Rilke's words—that God should grant everybody his own death argues in an essay entitled "Death and Laughter" (p. 591) that the whole image of Lechon and his creative path took on a different appearance and meaning and was distorted through his self-willed death. (Lechon was a practicing Roman Catholic. Z. Y.) Death revealed the real face of Lechon who had been famous for his wit and his charming and unnerving laughter— the face of a *poète maudit* (p. 591). Lechon was fascinated, bewitched by his own death. He carried on a combat with it, challenged it, perhaps flirted with it, as if he sought to render it harmless through his poetry (p. 592). "Like so many poets before him, he tried while still alive to intrude into another world *(Ibid.)*. But while the others paid only shorter or longer visits to that world, knowing that they would return to earth, Lechon behaved in the other world like a lodger, who, before renting for good a new apartment in an unknown place goes first to investigate the location of his new dwelling, its climate and conveniences and the general conditions under which he will have to live there" (p. 592). Wittlin quotes Lechon's poems in which he depicted not only "clear visions of his own death but also visions of his resurrection, realities for which he was preparing as a Christian aware of his sins and their consequences in the future life" (p. 592). Lechon kept company with death in a very humane way, he attempted to tame it as one might tame a wild beast, which one has for one reason or another to take home and which one knows will one day, in spite of our taming it, jump on us and tear us to pieces" (p. 593). At the end of the essay Wittlin quotes from a book by Maurice Blanchot, *L'Espace litteraire*, on the relationship between suicide and creativity. Blanchot maintains that suicide and the creativity of an artist are both subject to the same impulses and originate from similar ambitions. Both are forms of madness, despite the fact that the artist's experience is seemingly less fierce, less insane (p. 596). One could say that an artist is connected with his work in the same way that a human being is linked with death, which has also become his objective" (p. 596).

From Part IV we might also cite to the same effect an essay entitled "Hemingway, Death and Killing" in which Hemingway's relation to death is explored. (Wittlin begins by offering the generalization that writers have derived their knowledge about life, confronting it with death from the very beginnings of literature.) Hemingway seems to have looked for death to be his steady, lifelong companion as if he wished to provoke it to test its strength against his own (p. 622). Wittlin calls Hemingway a barbarian humanist who, while a friend of humanity, lived and died without God and without experiencing any impact of Christianity. . . .

Next to Wittlin's loyalty to Death stands his loyalty to all the Ultimate Things; i.e., to Heaven, Hell, Purgatory and the Last Judgment. This philosophical stance can easily be traced in nearly all of the numerous articles and essays in the book. What might be of more interest to the American reader is, however, Wittlin's preoccupation with suffering, which can be assigned a role next to Ultimate things and to Death. The themes of suffering and pain recur again and again throughout his reflections and generalizations. He calls passive and active suffering "the mother of art" (p. 60); he derives Rilke, "as every great artist" from suffering (p. 461) and we remember that in a youthful preface to his translation of the *Odyssey,* twice later reprinted, he defines Homer's Fatherland as pain (cf. chapter on the *Odyssey*). He is disappointed that the suffering endured during World War I did not ennoble mankind and concludes that Europeans "did not deserve this war" since it did not change them for the better (p. 80).

He speaks of "mortification and distress of the flesh" as "Heavensent" since they make the soul healthier (p. 236). He goes as far as to define the human soul—which he describes elsewhere as a "vestigial" organ of a human being, even putting it in quotation marks (cf. Preface)—as an organ which serves the human being for the sake of suffering (p. 474). As an artist he is interested more in sick souls than in healthy ones as for him what is within matters most. In one essay he draws an interesting comparison between Apollo and Asclepius; reminding the reader that Asclepius was a son of Apollo (p. 473) and establishing an interesting link between poets and physicians, who both look into the inward parts of men, he maintains that "when a man suffers the difference between body and soul is obliterated" (p. 475). He sees some similarity between the art of writing and the art of psychoanalysis in that the first brings relief through description of the suffering, even an exaggerating one, and the latter does so by uncovering the subconscious sources of suffering

(p. 475). He refers to the easing of pain by reproducing suffering in art as "the sublime mission of literature and its social meaning" (p. 475).

III   *Various Facets of a Portrait*

All these questions which we have brought up in connection with the search for persistent features in Wittlin's portrait do not amount to an exhaustive list and we could expand on them further. However, in addition to discussing the more constant features of his autobiography we would like to dwell upon certain features of the various aspects of his image as they emerge (we note that Wittlin's innate modesty prevents him from ever deliberately "exhibiting" these features) in the four parts of the book, which we shall call—the image of Wittlin the publicist in Part I, Wittlin the traveler in Part II, Wittlin the memorialist in Part III and Wittlin the literary critic and theater reviewer in Part IV. At the end we may be able to show how all these facets converge to give a unified portrait of one Wittlin, notwithstanding all the rich complexity and variety of the man and his long creative career.

In the first part of the book Wittlin comes before us as a pacifist and utopianist who believes—as most of the Expressionists did—that literature and art should assume the functions of religion. Poets who had suffered and searched for love during the horrible time of the First World War—says Wittlin in the article "War, Peace and a Poet's Soul" should be able to arouse "a hunger for love and peace in suffering humanity" (p. 35). He prays for peace using the words of the Holy Mass, and believes that poetry which is "building an enormous edifice of brotherhood and love" will help to bring about the radical change in the world which is so much needed. This youthful utopia of the keen young observer of the social and political scene in post-World War I Poland soon gave way to a more realistic view, to doubts about whether it would ever be possible to eliminate the causes of war in view of the fact that nobody is likely to renounce those of his earthly desires which come into collision with others' desires and aims and which, therefore, can only be defended by force. And only a change in morality would cause a real change in economic conditions. We soon realize that to Wittlin the moral side of human existence is one of its most interesting aspects. His concern for morality, and a moralizing tendency in his writings grows stronger as time passes. In the Preface to *Orpheus* he remarks that he witnessed many a moral defeat for mankind during his lifetime. He considers the 1930's, when Hitler came to power and Stalin carried out his spectacular trials and purges a fateful era for our common morality. He blames all alike for indifference and loss of sensitivity to others' suffering. He is concerned about collective morality and about the fact that such a morality seems at times nonexistent. Wittlin is a humanist (though he dislikes the word, cf. his essay "The Gift of Intellect," devoted to the brilliant Polish writer Herling-Grudzinski, not in *Orpheus*).[4] He is always concerned for human dignity and compassionate toward the least of men. In fact, he actually appealed for help for the hungry in 1934 at a time of widespread unemployment in Poland. Hunger and cold are to him not only social and economic phenomena, but also moral problems. He thinks that it is fortunate for human morality that no one's fate had been predetermined once and for all from cradle to grave. He poses the problem of the relationship between literature and society (cf. "The Last Resort," where the unemployed appealed to Wittlin as a well-known writer, showing thereby how seriously they took literature.) He still believes, with the Romantics, that a poet's words and deeds should coincide, and that the poet's word should exert power in life—a belief widespread in Eastern Europe.

Wittlin, who is simultaneously a broadly cosmopolitan and an intensely Polish writer, analyzes the state of Polish culture after World War I, pointing out not only its merits but its flaws and shortcomings with equal accuracy. He speaks out courageously against narrow nationalism, advocating a Polish national culture which can also play its due part in the symphony of world culture. He calls for a reassessment of traditional values for working out and forging a new culture which will make other nations aware of Poland as a member of the world cultural community and not just a land of suffering and heroic people. These earlier essays are supplemented by new ones, written during and after World War II outside of Poland.

As we have already noted, Wittlin was one of the editors of an *Anthology of Polish Democratic Thought*[5] published in New York in 1943 to which he contributed an "Epilogue" in which he

—always a true democrat—voiced his own democratic ideas and beliefs in very strong terms. Pointing to five centuries of the fight for justice and human dignity, for freedom and tolerance by Polish thinkers, writers and educators, Wittlin expresses the hope that this old and noble tradition will prevail in the end, and that words will finally be converted into deeds, that a new world will emerge out of words. . . . In the following year he was fighting again with words—his only weapon—against "Empty Words" (cf. pp. 124-26) such as "democracy," misused by those who have never had any democratic spirit. Some other contributions refer to the petty problems of émigré writers feuding with each other and call on them to make peace ("A New Year's Call to Concord" "Noworoczne wezwanie do zgody," p. 127). However, Wittlin has left his Polish and foreign readers something more than collections of émigré feuds. Part I of the *Orpheus* concludes with what Wittlin likes to call (in Thibaudet's phrase) a contribution to the "physiology" of literature in emigration.[6] It contains brilliant observations on the nature of writers and writing in exile and has been already favorably quoted by Harry Levin of Harvard.[7]

A true Christian, Wittlin reminds us of the use of the word "exile" in the beautiful antiphone "Salve Regina" where it refers to the whole of mankind, exiled from Paradise, whose earthly life is therefore considered an *exilium.* Then he brings in the fact of every writer's and poet's nonconformity with his environment, of his condition as an exile in his own country "because of his vocation" (p. 103). This makes members of the International P.E.N. Club in Exile like himself, not only double but triple exiles. . . . Wittlin considers this fact at once a misfortune and a privilege. Our loss of Paradise creates a proper distance from which we can view human affairs on earth *sub specie aeternitatis,* an angle of vision which particularly appeals to Wittlin. Thus for him the sorrow and grandeur of exile are intermingled. Depriving a writer of his native land, his language and his time (i.e., that time which is passing in his native country) is cruel and painful. However, great works of art have been created in complete isolation and solitude which is a more fertile soil for developing the gift of timeless vision. It is such a vision that enables the writer to produce eternal values and frees him from being imprisoned in his own time (p. 107). After all, exiled writers can only hope to write for posterity and if their hopes are to be fulfilled, then writing must contain some timeless, purely universal elements. Thus the story of the conquest of besieged Troy with the aid of a wooden horse is still relevant to us, who live in an atomic-hydrogen era (p. 111). The true mission of writers and artists is to give form and expression to the sublime "longings and presentiments of man," (p. 111) which are rooted in "some hazy memory of Paradise" to prepare "the soul of man for another existence no longer in exile" as did the anonymous artists of the Middle Ages who worked for the sake of the "holiness of their work" (p. 110).

IV   Travels. Europe

Part II of the *Orpheus* deals with Wittlin's impressions of travels in France, Italy, Yugoslavia, Austria and finally, in the United States. Wittlin is a very sophisticated traveler with a keen esthetic sense who looks at people, landscapes, bridges, monuments, museums with a fresh eye and has a great flair for rendering the *genius loci* of different countries and places. These sketches, in which one finds much *joie de vivre* are called *Stages;* stages in his curiosity, his eagerness to perceive and understand the world, to find the authenticity he is always seeking and to immortalize transient moments. His glance penetrates beneath the surface into the very soul of a city, a country, a nation, a landscape. He discerns in Italy a "terra mystica," where "the borders of faith fuse with the boundaries of art, where the content of a work of art becomes its form, the Christian humility is contained completely in the humility of the artist before his own craftsmanship" (p. 167). He speaks of Assisi, where the Middle Ages, so dear to him, have not yet been conquered by time only to exclaim a moment later, swayed by the beauty of the Italian landscape, that perhaps the Kingdom of God was from this world as well. . . . Although he poses in the *Stages* as a reporter, a "counterfeit reporter" would perhaps be a better expression, he offers us a highly individual vision of places, men and events. Indeed, his is the "super-reporter's truth" (p. 524), the inner, hidden truth and meaning of facts and phenomena. He is interested above all in the emotional aura of things, their individual coloring, which he tries, almost always successfully, to evoke for his reader. The places he sees, the cities he visits, are distinctively colored by his hypersensitivity, his dynamism of emotion, his hunger for truth and authenticity, his striving to defamiliarize things which have lost their meaning and expressiveness because too many eyes have seen them only through Baedecker, to whom he devotes a brilliant essay in the *Stages*. He himself never follows Baedecker, never treads well-beaten paths, but always looks for a way of his own in both the direct and the metaphorical sense. (That is why he is such a brilliant essayist!) The spirit of negation (of banal and worn-out clichés) has played no less a part in the creation of these unusual travel sketches than have Wittlin's gift for delighted admiration and his ability to stir our interest by bringing out rich and unexpected associations—associations which display not only his enormous erudition and the enchanting play of his poet's imagination, but also an amazing empathy which allows him not only to write of what Marie Antoinette might have seen from the window of her prison (when he describes his fascinating trips underneath all the bridges of Paris—he loves bridges for the same reason he loves all Borderlands) but what her thoughts might have been as she gazed out of that window. Paris—as Wittlin's witty aphorism would have it—is not like one's first kiss, but rather like the first cigarette one smokes. The city does not immediately evoke exaltation, one has to grow into it and absorb it with one's sensitivity so that one can at length, like Wittlin, say that it is in Paris that the traveler learns that life should not be taken too tragically, but not too lightly and idyllically either, that all men, even ex-dictators are at home on the streets of Paris, that children and elderly people alike make us feel their link with the earth; the former because they have not yet grown far enough from it, the latter because they are beginning to grow back into it again. Wittlin feels "literature in the very air of Paris," the city which was first shown to him by his dear friend Joseph Roth and here he gives us, seemingly quite casually, a thorough account of contemporary French prose. I believe that what Wittlin has written in "Grandeur and Sorrows of Exile" about those imponderable things which the writer in exile loses does not really apply to him: he knows how to capture at least some of these imponderables, the visible and invisible realities of each place he has liked. It is as if love has disclosed to him what is usually revealed only to native observers. His glance turns inward, especially in his rendering (one hesitates to call it a "description") of the Cathedral of Chartres as an integral microcosm, "a capital of the genius of Western Christianity" (p. 198). Here he not only gives us many proofs of his acute and perceptive appreciation of all kinds of art, but guides us toward an understanding of our own inward relation to the phenomenon of Chartres for, he says, what we take away from Chartres is not the only important thing but what we bring with us to the experience, even though everything we bring will necessarily seem insignificant in the face of this genuine greatness. "We are, as it were, in the capital, in the very center of the zone where man's thought about God comes into contact with God's thought on man" (p. 197). Such concise aphoristic statements are characteristic of Wittlin's style both as a poet and as a traveler. One could call his style here a poetic sort of reportage with some novelistic elements which to a certain extent transfigures "so called" (as Wittlin likes to call it) reality, uncovering its deeper levels of meaning and finding hidden inner relationships between various phenomena. Another good example of this is his description of the exhibition of works by the famous sculptor Ivan Mestrovic in Yugoslavia. He is not afraid to compare the Moses by Mestrovic with Michaelangelo's Moses and says that Mestrovic's sculpture can sustain the comparison favorably. He deems Mestrovic's Yugoslavian Venus comparable to Venus of Milo (p. 220).

Wittlin's description of the exhibition effectively contributes to our understanding of that complex subject, the soul of the Southern Slavs. Enraptured by Mestrovic's works, he asks himself: "Reporter, what is happening to you? Where is your professional reserve? The reporter is no more—he has vanished during Mestrovic's exhibit!" (p. 220). And in general, the author of the *Stages,* except in a few places, does not sound like a professional reporter. Usually he not only succeeds in discovering the inner truth of phenomena, but in formulating that truth as well. Is it his myth-making imagination, which is apparent here, that helps to make everything alive and part of an organic system of that Beauty which is Truth and Truth which is Beauty? This mythic imagination colors his style very distinctly in the poetic and epic genres and it also colors his travel sketches. It is present, for example, in his account of a visit paid to Vienna just before Hitler's *Anschluss* when he sought to recover his former self of

twenty years earlier. Suddenly, the whole atmosphere of a bygone time which he had believed would survive only in the pages
of *The Salt of the Earth* came alive for him again as he wandered
the streets of the once-gay "waltz-tune" city. It is Wittlin's imagination and his masterly handling of language even in "reportage" that gives everything he writes about, a wonderful
unity and originality.

V *The U. S. A.*

The final sketches of the Part II of the *Orpheus* are devoted
to the U. S. A., to Wittlin's first steps in and impressions of this
country. In an essay entitled "What kind of America did I come
to?" he says:

I did not come to the land of millionaires or gangsters or movie stars.
I was going to the America of free men: white, black and yellow, and
to the descendants of "The Last of the Mohicans." My guides in this
long journey, the result of a sad "historical necessity" were the poets
and writers who haunted our European childhood and youth. (p. 278)

The first book he bought in the United States was Walt Whitman's *Leaves of Grass*. He mentions other American writers who
were the "friends" and "eternal companions" of his youth: Har-
riet Beecher Stowe, Fenimore Cooper, Mark Twain, Poe and
Emerson. He admits that the romantic America, whose image
was created by their books was very different from the real
America he saw as an émigré writer. However, he has managed
to preserve some feeling for the America of his childhood, for
the "country of liberty, simplicity and brotherhood" (p. 279).

In an essay entitled "My First Year in America" he speaks of
the "derailing of Europe" during the last war, a derailing which
had its consequence in the arrival of a new wave of émigrés in
the United States. He points out that among these newcomers
there were those who often demanded more of this country than
they did of themselves, and who easily forgot that in coming
here they have been enabled to save their creative freedom and
their dignity. "We should be grateful to a country in which
thought and creativity are not only free, but are held in esteem
only when they are free"—he exclaims (p. 283). He praises
American schools which bring happiness to children and not

misery, like the schools of his childhood and youth. He presents
a short survey of the American literary scene, calling American
literature "one of the most original" in the world. Next to Bernard
Shaw and Maeterlinck, Eugene O'Neill is, according to Wittlin,
the most outstanding dramatist in the sphere of modern Western
civilization. He concludes by calling for freedom of mind and
conscience in keeping with best American tradition (p. 291).

Another essay on America eulogizes and surveys the Latin
elements in the language and the cultural make-up of New York.
It is entitled "Novi Eboraci," which means "in New York in
Latin. Wittlin reminds the reader that America received a
ready-made culture from England in the seventeenth century and
that the first American writers resembled in many ways the
English humanists of that time. Summarizing in brief the story
of American literature he stresses its elements drawn from the
classical heritage and sketches the story of its gradual emanci-
pation. He notes with satisfaction the return of a taste for classical
antiquity in the works of Ezra Pound, T. S. Eliot and Hilda
Doolittle to whom this is "an inner region of defense and escape,"
in Doolittle's words (p. 308).

Part II of the *Orpheus* ends with a brilliant essay on Edgar
Allan Poe in the Bronx, which appeared in English translation in
the *Polish Review,* Vol. VI, No. 1-2 (Winter-Spring, 1959). Here
Poe and his little white house in the Bronx are dramatically contrasted with the Bronx's contemporary inhabitants, mainly Jews
of Polish origin to whom the very name of Poe means nothing.
Wittlin calls the Bronx "a Jewish paradise on Earth." At the end
of the essay he vividly describes the preparations in the Bronx on
the eve of Yom Kippur. With a wonderful associative and evocative power he summons up an image of Poe looking at a drunkard
in the street, who lies bleeding there without attracting anyone's
attention. The recollection of Poe's death spurs the writer to
exclaim: "Oh, Lord! Thou who judgest the souls of both Jews
and non-Jews—be merciful to the inhabitants of the Bronx!" Thus
an essay which opens with a poignant portrayal of a particular
place, ends—as is so often the case with Wittlin—in a look "beyond" at those timeless values with which he is primarily concerned.

VI   My Lwów

Part III of the *Orpheus* consists mainly of the little book, *My Lwów*, earlier published separately. It is a colorful tale (*gaweda*, "conversational narrative," a favorite genre in the Polish literary tradition) of his favorite city, the city of which he likes to consider himself a native. It is an intimate account of everything in Lwów which appealed to Wittlin and which his memory has preserved. He strains every nerve to achieve the utmost truthfulness and sincerity, and, therefore, calls his memory a "falsifier" but we may be grateful to it for having preserved for us not only scenes but voices, colors, and smells of the beautiful city of Wittlin's youth. His remarkable talent has fused a thousand small details and striking features into an organic whole, to evoke the very soul of his city. The sight of Lwów, its magnificent churches and monuments, its beautiful streets and parks are recreated for us by the author. The facts of Wittlin's own life are interspersed with information about the life of celebrities he knew in Lwów; the historical and geographical features of the city are permeated with the aura of the past, adorned with legend and myth interwoven with anecdotes, gossip, snatches of old popular songs. . . . Wittlin gives us the history of the city from an unusual angle, from inside out, as it were, where intangible things figure prominently, perhaps even more prominently, than the tangible ones. Wiktor Weintraub has compared *My Lwów* to *Portraits souvenirs* by Jean Cocteau adding, however, that the former displays its own unique features.[8] For him Lwów is a city of the shadows of all who perished so tragically during the terrible conflicts of our century. He can still sense there "the people who have long since stopped walking about." He describes poignantly a promenade of the shadows of the dead on Lwów's famous Corso where "the officers of the Austrian Dragoons with monocles in the empty sockets of what once were their eyes clank about with their spurs, where the Ukrainian nationalists of 1918 are walking arm-in-arm with the Polish defenders of Lwów" (p. 358). Is it Wittlin's intimacy with the dead that makes everything in *My Lwów* come miraculously alive, even people "from stone and bronze," who are brought down from their pedestals through the technique of defamiliarizing them (such as Mickiewicz's monument, for instance), or linking them with some small but telling detail from more recent times? I do not know, but I do know that the gamut of colors, sounds and smells which the author of *My Lwów* succeeded in evoking and recreating can never be forgotten by any of his readers, whether they were born in Lwów or "initiated" into it by this masterly evocation of the one-time spirit of a wonderful city, which is now only a legend.

VII   *More Travels in Time . . .*

This part of *Orpheus* is rounded out by three other sketches written in the same vein: "A View from the Window" (about Montreal, Canada), "First Impressions from the Theater," and "A Few Words on Muck" (a sick dog). "The View from the Window" vies with *My Lwów* in its colorfulness, "recall" of the spirits, sounds and smells and melodious prose. In Montreal a neoclassic building (St. Sulpice's Seminary) and snow make Wittlin "see" a similar eighteenth-century building of an exmonastery he had known in Lwów as a hospital. The author does not go back to Lwów of the past, but rather summons this past to him as one would in a lyrical poem. He says: the building "has sailed over to me across the Atlantic Ocean, has loomed up out of the precipice of time and stands in the park . . . in Montreal" (pp. 367-68). Montreal and Lwów interweave in the nostalgic soul of the observer; past and present, life and literature, history and myth at first overlap, then fuse into an expressive whole:

In the snowstorm, the heads of Iroquois Indians appear before me with their colorful feathers. The picturesque names of the many tribes of the family Algonquin—Nipissing, Temiskaming, Ottawa, Missisanga —sing in my ears like the colorful trimmings of their headdress. The snow itself takes on the color of these feathers and these names. The redskins swing their tomahawks—as in the circus of Buffalo Bill [which Wittlin attended as a child in Lwów, Z.Y.] and shooting arrows from their bows they aim straight at the lighted windows of St. Sulpice's Seminary. The snowstorm quiets down and clusters around white, immobile shrouds; and once more it is Lwów. . . . It snows again— quietly, monotonously, sleepily as at the end of James Joyce's story "The Dead." (pp. 372-73)

The snow covers the buildings and orchards of Lwów and Montreal. "And it covers us too—the last, the very last of the Mohicans." The above quotation might afford us at least a glimpse into the intricate art of evocation and into the soul of an exile. In the Preface to the *Stages*, Wittlin referred to two great writers of the twentieth-century who knew how to satisfy their hunger after cognizing the world. He contrasted Joseph Conrad-Korzeniowski—"a traveler in space," as he called him, with Marcel Proust, "a traveler in time," who liked to explore depths of the human soul. Wittlin's memoirs and impressions may endear him to the native reader not less than Proust's, especially because of the familiarity of the associational and emotional aura. Moreover, they might be looked upon as a contribution to the "physiology of literature in exile," a field inaugurated by Wittlin with his essay "Sorrow and Grandeur of Exile," which was briefly analyzed by us. We hope that the writer will further explore this virtually unknown territory, satisfying his own and our "hunger for authenticity."

VIII　*A Literary and Theatrical Critic*

In Part IV of *Orpheus* Wittlin emerges as a very discerning and erudite literary critic with an eye for metaphysical profundities. The stamp of his powerful intellect lies on all his acute analyses of various cultural and intellectual phenomena. We find more essays and book reviews dealing not only with contemporary literature, with modern books which have attracted him, with writers of various nationalities some of whom were his personal friends, but important contributions to the history of ideas of the past which he knows how to relate to our present concerns. Thus the name and the works of St. Augustine are mentioned next to those of Barbusse and Bernanos; Stendhal keeps company with Joseph Roth and Gerhart Hauptmann, St. Francis, Rilke and Gogol are his eternal "fellow-travelers" and companions. Wyspianski, Jan Stur, Kasprowicz, Ostap Ortwin, Franciszek Fiszer, though less well known internationally are of even more importance as his friends and predecessors, as are lifelong friends like Joseph Roth and Hermann Kesten, or Tuwim and Lechon. An index to *Orpheus*, which unfortunately does not exist, would include hundreds of more or less illustrious names. But Wittlin is no mere "namedropper." Behind his reflections, comments and generalizations one always senses the presence of an erudite and brilliant essayist who knows how to probe

everything he investigates and how to express his original outlook in a most concise and witty fashion. For example, two
articles in *Orpheus* are devoted to Gogol, one written on the
100th anniversary of that writer's death, the other describing
Wittlin's impressions of Julian Tuwim's 1934 dramatization in
Warsaw of Gogol's celebrated "Overcoat." Wittlin immediately
seizes upon a most important aspect of Gogol's creativity which
helps us to understand him better; i.e., the part played by the
devil in Gogol's work. Wittlin calls Gogol's laughter infernal—
a laughter which originated in Hell. He singles out three aspects
which were reflected alike in Gogol's soul and in his art: Fear,
the Absurd and Boredom (Ennui). He applies to Gogol what
Blake once said of Milton: that Milton was really "of the Devil's
party." Characteristically, the article (available also in an Italian
translation, cf. Bibliography) is entitled "Gogol's Inferno." In
the second article, on the "Overcoat" Wittlin, in addition to an
expert theatrical review with unrestrained praise for the fine
Polish actor Stefan Jaracz, stresses the role the old tailor Petrovich
played in the wretched Akakii Akakievich's fate. It is the role
of a devil or at least so it was performed by Jaracz. It is interesting to note that about the same time—and Wittlin did not know
this—an Italian translation of Gogol's "Overcoat" contained an
illustration which depicted Petrovich with . . . horns!

The theater is of great interest to Wittlin who also now continues to review American theater performances for Polish
listeners over Radio Free Europe. But even here he is interested
primarily in the zone where the Creator is in touch with nature—
in the confrontation between man and God. He sees the theater
as a place for mystical rites (cf. his essay "The Empty Theater"
and later pronouncements) where God is at once a Spectator
and an omniscient Judge (p. 389). Thus, in the essay entitled
"St. Augustine and the Theater" (p. 390 ff.), he singles out a
chapter from St. Augustine's *Confessions* dealing with the Roman
theater, which the saint condemned, criticizing Aristotle's theory
of catharsis and finding the theatrical arts immoral *per se*. Wittlin sees St. Francis of Assisi as the initiator of a new Christian
outlook upon the morality of the theater, since he introduced a
Christmas play to Greccio, a town which had once been a part
of the Roman Empire's territory (p. 393).

IX   *Joseph Wittlin and Joseph Roth*

As far as an autobiography, or even material for an autobiography is concerned, Wittlin writes surprisingly little about himself. He is too modest for that. He tells us very little about his childhood and youth—usually, by the way, that part of a person's life to which biographers, if not autobiographers devote the least space—and also very little about his development as a poet and writer. He very seldom writes directly about himself, except in *My Lwów*. But in his tributes to dead friends like Jan Stur or Joseph Roth we find glimpses of Wittlin the man and the artist. For example, in an essay entitled "A Reminiscence of Joseph Roth,"[9] we find some of his own Viennese reminiscences, references to Karl Kraus as a teacher, Wittlin's reasons for entering the Austro-Hungarian Army, etc. Wittlin calls Roth "a friend of his soul" as he, too, was called by Roth. Indeed, they had much in common. A large part of Roth's biography belongs to Wittlin's life story as well (p. 506). Wittlin calls Roth a visionary, a prophet of catastrophe who was trying to warn people of an impending Apocalypse. He sees him also as the first writer in German literature who portrayed the moral catastrophe which befell the participants of World War I. One wishes that he had written still more such warm, heartfelt essays, if only to allow us to glean some more facts on Wittlin himself. His ability to praise and admire others—not just himself as so many other modern writers do—is no less significant. He himself has stressed this quality in Boris Pasternak to whom he has devoted three essays.

X   *A "Religious Man"*

It would be extremely difficult to reconstruct a consistent world-view out of the great variety and number of these essays, articles, memoirs, speeches and addresses; out of the veritable flood of valuable observations, profound reflections, generalizations and comments, especially since *Orpheus* comprises forty years of an eventful and mentally intense life. However, if one were to ask what one quality pervades all these manifestations of high critical intelligence over a period of several decades, and imparts unity to them one would probably have to answer that it is the outlook of a profoundly "religious man" ("Der religiöse Mensch," Spranger's term),[10] who sees the world *sub specie*

mortis and endeavors always to write in *articulo mortis,* even
when he treats not of grave things, but of gay. It is also the work
of a Christian existentialist, who, although one dreads to apply
such ready-made labels to such a complex poet and writer, is
convinced that man's soul, which in our times is in danger of
complete annihilation, should be saved, that human goodness
and righteousness as opposed to wickedness—in the Biblical sense
of these terms—should be believed in, even if only "on credit."
Wittlin emerges from this book as a highly perceptive observer
of the social and political, and especially of the cultural and
literary scene, and as a writer of absolute integrity who is concerned only to find and reveal the truth. What cements all this
varied material in various genres together, is his unique personality, his critical intelligence directed by moral sense and moral
passion. This passion, together with his Christian longing for
justice, unites the many facets of Wittlin we encounter in the
book into the one Wittlin whose highly integrated personality
and moralist's stance are perhaps best expressed in his literary
style. One can observe here not only changes in his convictions
and opinions but also changes in his style as it becomes with the
passage of time more and more polished, witty, aphoristic and
subtle. Wittlin was one of the first to practice the difficult art of
the essay in Poland and remains one of the few contemporary
masters of the form there. His insights into the "lining of human
existence," his own expression (Z. Y.) into literary works and
works of art in general, become ever deeper as time passes and
his fine understanding of "la condition humaine" becomes more
exact. What he says in his article on Mickiewicz's great epic *Pan
Tadeusz* (which is available in English translation)[11] could be
applied equally well to himself in *Orpheus.* He maintained in
this article that the development of reportage, photography, the
movies, radio and television has forced modern writers to abandon the surfaces of life (p. 528) and to head into its deeper
realms. It has made them express in words only the things which
they could not express by any other means of communication.
His credo is that the world appears as it has been presented by
great poets—and not by reporters—as it was seen by El Greco,
Rembrandt, and Cezanne—and not by photographers. His own
literary and essayistic art are an ample argument for and fulfill-
ment of this credo.

CHAPTER 7

Tentative Conclusions

S INCE Joseph Wittlin's writing career is still continuing ac-
tively, it would be, of course, premature to draw any final
conclusions about his work, and the following general remarks
are necessarily of only a tentative nature.

As a poet Wittlin is primarily important as a Polish Expressionist, among whom he ranks as first in stature. It has been stated
by outstanding specialists in the field that he was the only Polish
Expressionist who was able to represent Polish Expressionism
adequately to European literature.[1] There is no economy in Wittlin's early *Hymns,* everything is dominated by emotion, and
subject to its eruptive power. The choice of words, images, exclamations, repetitions, pauses, suspension points—all are used
by the author in order to intercept an emotional vision of the
world and bring it close to the reader, and even infect him with
it. The use of images is often rhetorical or ornamental; the poet
can be accused here of vehemence and verbosity. However, even
today this uninterrupted flow of words usually captivates and
carries away the reader. In view of these features of his early
poetry, Wittlin's later economy, almost austerity as in his classical
"Stabat Mater" or "To the Polish Language" is all the more
surprising. The poetry of the later period is condensed, displaying
high emotional and intellectual "charge." The late poetry of the
1960's is of a different kind, one which could be termed "tales,"
gaweda (conversational narrative) in verse. Wittlin's poetry has
been attentively read by Polish poets of the younger generation.
Volume II of Wittlin's *Works* which is to be published by Instytut
Literacki of *Kultura* in Paris, will be devoted to his poetry.

Just as in the early 1920's Wittlin managed to command attention and to take his place in the front rank of Independent
Poland's young poets, so in the 1930's he managed to write what

is justly regarded as "one of the best novels of the *interbellum* period."[2] *The Salt of the Earth* is a permanent addition to literature in all the thirteen languages into which it has been translated. This has been clearly demonstrated by the dramatic revival of the novel in Germany and Austria, where it was acclaimed "the book of the month" in the summer of 1969. Termed a predecessor of the "nouveau roman" of France by such discerning critics as the German writer Hermann Kesten[3] it is today winning more and more praise from German and Austrian readers. Although I have not mentioned the "nouveau roman" in my chapters on *The Salt of the Earth,* it should be obvious from their contents that *The Salt of the Earth* is a far cry from a traditional novel and that it stands much closer to a plotless novel in which situations and things are more important than people. *The Salt of the Earth* has left its traces in contemporary Polish prose as everyone who is familiar with Julian Stryjkowski's *Austeria (The Inn)*[4] will agree.

What of Wittlin as the translator of the *Odyssey?* Which *Odyssey,* Wittlin's poetic rendering or Parandowski's prose text will become the Polish *Odyssey?* This question cannot be answered at present. Sometimes it is necessary to wait for centuries for any adequate translation of a familiar classic. The Poles were fortunate enough to have received two first-class versions of the *Odyssey* within a short period of time. Only the future will show which translation will triumph and only in the event that Wittlin's *Odyssey* is freely admitted into Poland.

As for Wittlin's critical articles and essays, items he himself considers "marginal" in his creative output, read perceptively they cannot fail to astonish the reader with their extraordinary rich content and refined form. Wittlin the critic and essayist is original, witty, always keeping to his own path, and passes judgment with unerring taste and foresight, as in the case of Witold Gombrowicz (1904-1969).[5] Wittlin's erudition is impressive, and his range of interest vast. He is a humanist in both the old and the new sense of the word; but more than that he is a moralist, for whom (as Kierkegaard put it) "irony is only an incognito."[6] A moralist's passion and a humanist's heart direct his critical intelligence. And he is also an existentialist, a "frustrated friend of humanity" (as he once confided to me), but still a friend!

Wittlin's Poems in Translation

Prelude

Within me still shriek perishing battalions,
A memory alive with loudly shattered thrones.
And breathless again I come rushing to you
Burdened with the load of harvest new.

Within my lungs, gas, dust, the world ablaze,
Still strangle each word that forms in my throat.
O, how sublime the grace of God
That I crossed these seas of blood
To you, kind people.

Like a ghastly nightmare pressing on my chest,
The black day I recall—forgetting, yet seeing.
Today is purgatory—yesterday was hell;
Endure, my friends, till evening endure.
Tomorrow Eden comes into being.

I am still struggling, for within me complains
All Europe. Within me she raises her fist heavenward
In protest: a mankind of slaves,
With all the crosses of all wars' graves.
She starts, threatens, and clamors.

But tomorrow, enraptured, she'll extend her hands
Toward heaven; for she knocked not in vain:
Manna is falling, and refreshing dew.
Life, bitter, sweetens again.

(Trans. D. M.)

To the Adversary

How heavily breathes our day!
Tediously it groans in the struggle
Waged by the spirit's effort.

In tumult of people and daily affairs
We forge murderous arms.
With a visor we tightly cover our faces,
Menacing to the eye of the beholder.

Heralds already sound their trumpets—
The time to attack has come,
And with a fierce battle cry
We advance upon each other from opposite sides.
As on an ancient stone relief
Portraying heated battles,
In a melee of primitively carved bodies,
Bent torsos, hands, and short swords,
In desperate thrust of shields extended
And frenzied, twisted faces—
We advance: terrible, violent.
Behind us countless soldiers,
Enthralled tribes.

Behold! Two armies locked in deadly combat,
As on an ancient stone relief.
Spears clash against helmets,
Wounded moan, felled by the sword;
Masses of massacred bodies shrivel
Amidst rattling armor.

On shields proudly glitter our emblems,
Each extolling its own legend.
We cast at each other stones of invective;
Venom flows freely from our lips.
Intoxicated with the rage of battle,
The smell of flesh and flowing blood
We speed over corpses of conflicting thoughts,
And spur on frothing steeds
To trample our whirling thoughts.
Two invisible adversaries, concealed
Behind visors slammed shut.

All day corpses tumble about;
All day continues our awful fight.
Horses snort, people pant
Amidst torn bodies, aquiver in death,
As on an ancient stone relief.

Soon our day grows weary of battle,
Gives way to night ascending.
We walk to rest in quiet tents:
My enemy undaunted, and I.

We walk in sorrow, silent, lost in thought
Of our reason for this dire struggle,
Of our toil of untiring war,
Waged, perhaps, all our lives
For some holy and noble cause.

This moment, gripped by boundless sadness,
When calm quenches senses inflamed,
We suddenly stop before our tents:
My bloody opponent and I.
Each puts his hand on his overflowing heart—
Together, at once, we become aware
That it is for one and the same cause
We fight each other all through life:
For the one, unnamed, sacred
Cause.

Thus we linger, both, at once:
Hand on heart, tall, motionless—
I on my side—he on his.
(Both armies spent; succumbed to slumber.)
We stand; two hot, immaculately clear
Living tears fallen from the eyes of God,
Oblivious to one another.

(Trans. D. M.)

Hymn to Hands

Speak softly.
This instant when my soul
Slumbers with eyes half open,
All over this earth
Millions of hands are moving.

O hands, hands, generous hands!
O hands, hands, laboring hands!
O hands, two living curses!

And those which hurt, and those which kill,
And the ones which experience all feeling;

And fragile hands, virginal white,
Which await motherhood, and tranquil, lie still—
And those which scream and howl like dogs,
And the ones which whimper like a babe in a cradle,
And the hands with which poets inspired
And holy masters of all creation
Untired, mold their wondrous worlds,
O hands:
This adoration is for you.

O hands—stinging whips; O hands—shovels digging;
O palms—hearts open; fingers—poems asleep.
Hands—legends, and like lizards, fickle;
Courageous divers of oceans deep!
Rakes for a miser piling up his treasure,
Magic wands bringing forth longing beyond measure,
When one strikes the dormant strings.
Hands—thunders!

Books recondite for the sage to ponder
Truths eternal! Weepers for a father standing
At the grave of his only daughter:
O greed never satiated!

You two fondling, yearning tunes
Softly caressing aching brows!
Snow-white angelic wings, in compassion,
Spread over human woes!

———————————————

O, how my hands ache
As I write these words!

Speak softly!
A million hands tell me their tales
Of each injustice, of each foul deed,
Each joy sustaining man's very soul.

All transient forms on earth
Human hands mold, create—
I feel a searing breath: Eternity,
Which human hands cannot destroy.

Though wherever I turn, forward or back,
Wherever I look, whether far or near—
Speak softly!
Behind me forever moves a spectre—hands.
Speak softly!
Behind me forever glides a phantom—fear.

(Adapted version by D. M.)

The People in the Streetcar

All the people in the streetcar
Drown in the same newspapers.
Let's glance at their faces:
At this moment they look
Like born criminals.

Through ice-cold eyes, into all their brains,
The same evil news creeps
Each soul wallows in the same mire;
All rejoice
That someone was murdered,
That someone was arrested,
That someone else, not they, tomorrow at dawn
will be hanged.

(Trans. D. M.)

An Ode in Honor of the Polish Language and Polish Poetry

Glory to you, humble slaves and servants of my mother tongue:
Pronouns, prepositions, adverbs—quiet and submissive.
Without your aid could Mickiewicz have been Mickiewicz?
Or Jan Czarnoleski the lutanist inspired?

And glory to you, paupers without soul or splendor:
Tiny dots above "ż," modest accents under "a,"
Only one, the Polish language and its anguished song
Endows you with grace.

Glory to you, churls trailing after lordly retinues:
Prosaic, toiling words, well-worn, like old coins—
Barely a touch of a poet's loving hand
Renders you ablaze, holy, like Sinai's bush.

Glory to you, winged chargers of the royal stud,
On whom bards, by assault, conquered gates of heaven;

But you, too, beloved, lowly peasant horses, awaits
An abundance of oats and four-leafed clovers.

Glory to you, sinless, benevolent thieves of fire divine,
Blessed be the vultures who torment your bodies;
For, "flame will devour pictorial history . . .
The song will escape whole - - -"

(Trans. D. M.)

A Lullaby for my Baby Daughter

Black men's black hands pick for you,
My fair one, green bananas.
For you, across vast oceans,
Large ships to Gdynia sail—

You sleep and know nothing.

Each day before the morning star
Routs troops of darkness in bloody combat,
Somewhere, far away, someone is milking
Snow-white milk, for you.

And you smile in your sleep.

Incomprehensible sounds like missiles
Strike the ramparts of your cradle.
The armor of nescience, like a tender nurse,
Shields your soul with gentle quietude.

And you float on the wave of time.

Before you awaken, disturbed in your sleep
By a painful plaint of white people like you;
Before the bull led to slaughter bellows for you;
Before you learn that all sweetness is bitter—

Sleep, and know nothing.

(Trans. D. M.)

Litany

About all that now occurs—I am silent.
I am silent about my fellow-men degraded.
I am silent about my fellow-men disgraced.

I am silent about Poland after the Marshal's death,
About the hunger of the hungry and the satiety of the satiated.
About all those vanquished in unequal battle.
I am silent about village squalor and the peasant's fate.
I am silent about city squalor and unemployment.
I am silent about darkness in the souls of the oppressors.
I am silent about darkness in the souls of the oppressed.
I am silent about pitting people against people.
I am silent about thrashings of the weak and the defenseless,
And about the existence of Bereza Kartuska,
And about chains on the poet's hands.
(I am silent about you too, Mr. Censor—
Hence do not confiscate my silence.)

I am silent about all that renders my conscience
An impure, bleeding, purulent wound.
I am silent about all that strangles my throat.
I am silent about nightmares laid by night
On my heart full of dread and bitterness—
From gates of hells flung open
The soul cries out in silence.
I am silent about the maleficence I behold.
I am silent about all armed cowards,
About tons of blood spilled in vain.
I am silent about wars already in progress.
I am silent about wars to erupt tomorrow.
I am silent about children in the Madrid mortuary.
I am silent about the boon of bombs and of mustard gas.
I am silent about all Moscow trials.
I am silent about Satan who roams the world.

O Lord! Judge of my words and deeds,
May the penalty for my silence not be harsh.

(Trans. D. M.)

Stabat Mater

The sorrowing mother stood upon the square,
And saw her dead son's body hanging there.

She stood within the world's unfeeling space
A kerchief framed the Polish mother's face.

She does not speak a single word, nor cries
But fixes the cold corpse with stony eyes.

He hangs there barefoot, lonely and bereft,
(The Germans took his shoes before they left.)

And in her son's shoes they would march along,
Tramping the soil which they had come to wrong.

Tramping the martyred soil they hold in fee,
That waits and watches, silent now as she.

         ✿   ✿   ✿

Stabat Mater, Mater dolorosa Thou,
They've cut Thy sons down from the gallows now.

Thou layest each to rest in the murky tomb,
Dead, lifeless fruit of Thy most sacred womb.

Stabat Mater, Mater Nostra fair,
Polonia! Thine the crown of thorns to wear.

(Trans. Elizabeth Clark Reiss)

To the Polish Language

All you could give, you have given us, Lord,
Of our song, wrath, lamentation.
You went into exile together with us.
Oh, grant us now the last sacraments.

White dove of the silent covenant
Between those who are free and those defeated,
Fly down to the stalags. In a soldiers mouth
Live! You, at least, appease his desire!

Like milk and honey, flow into ghastly gutters
Of cities stricken with temporal bondage.
In the sweetest of all words, bid farewell to corpses
Of those slain in the open field.

And when we return to the gory bosom,
Where you and we had our nascence—
In Polish silence may angels greet
The martyred land.

(Trans. D. M.)

Lament XX

Smuggling its rays through the linden leaves the July sun,
Like a faithful dog, licks my poor head and hands.
I'll give up all sweetness, comfort and friends
For your glance—just one.

I had many buddies for jugs of sweet wine!
Who can count the readers of my poignant song today?
You that wish to share this bitter cup, pray.
Where are you, friend of mine?

Most laughable in this great pain, I sit alone.
I polish rhymes of Niobe, don't howl despair.
To cry like simple men I mustn't dare.
Ursula, my own?

The meanest hand who turns my country sod
Can take his little child upon his knee.
I guess you've made him happier than me,
O potent God!

Each night his children eat with him, content
With macaroni, wooden spoon, and common bowl.
But I?—Like an aged clown I play my role,
Write a lament.

O great and cruel Muses, O Apollo, Sire!
Let my sorrow forget Niobe's mood!
Oh if on Ursula's stony grave I could
Shatter you, my lyre!

(Trans. Adam Gillon)

Lament of a Sacrificial Ram

Why me? Because I am an animal
and have no soul? Because my horns have got
entangled fast in a thorny thicket
so that I could not run away
from the old man crazed with fear?

Their wisemen say that since the sixth day
of world's Creation I have been waiting
on Mount Moriah for that knife
so that my throat be cut and not the boy's,

so that instead of him upon the wood
I burned.

The obedient patriarch fed the fire
with aromatic roots, resin, incense,
nard and myrtle—not to offend Him
who asked the ancient father for such a horrid
sacrifice, spare Him the smell of my burning
innards, the stench of my injustice crying
to the heavens—
     And He was pleased with
the smoke of my pain, aroma of my agony.
Does it matter that I have no soul
although my body feels the same anguish
they do, and my heart thumps as fast
from fear as theirs quail and freeze
when the angel of death flutters his wings?

Was it necessary to have the sacrifice?
Was it not enough to toy with the patriarch's heart,
to quench His thirst for blind obedience?
Why could he not have spared my life as well?
To make good use of wood for burnt offerings?
to keep the rust off the knife unstained by my blood?
He counted too much on my ignorance.
for I have no soul—
     Yes, animals
have no souls hence they cannot sin.
We were not banished
from paradise
     —And you, what have you made
of your soul? A poisoned cistern
in which your sundry crimes are nurtured.
If only this: that your innocent must always
suffer, perish for the guilty ones.

Whole nations of two-legged scapegoats
endowed with souls burn in crematoria,
foul fumes beat against the vaults of heavens
and yet no angels fly downward
to stay the hangman's hands from murder.

And the wisemen say: the fire failed
to consume all of me on Mount Moriah;

upon my bones, they say, a temple
was built for Him; of my arteries
they wove the strings for David's harp
and my skin was used for a belt by Elijah
the prophet who shall trumpet on
the Mountain of Moriah, blowing
my right horn (filed and drilled out)
when the prayed-for Messiah at last comes
to the descendants of the meek patriarch.

....

Oh, blow at both my horns
under the Wailing Wall,
                    my pain does not count,
my fear is of no import, for I have no soul.
And only once in this earth's annals
the animals were called brothers—by a holy man.

                              (Trans. Adam Gillon)

Notes and References

Chapter One

1. *Hymny.* (Poznan: Nakl. Zdroju, 1920); 2nd edition (Warsaw, 1927); 3rd edition (Warsaw: J. Mortkowicz, pod znakiem poetów. Seria nowa, 1929).

2. *Oficyna poetów i malarzy* (Poets' and Painters' Press) No. 1 (12), (London, 1969), pp. 2-8.

3. *The Salt of the Earth* came out in German for the first time in Amsterdam: *Das Salz der Erde* (Allert de Lange, 1937) trans. Dr. I. Berman, Preface by Joseph Roth. It had been prohibited in Germany before the Second World War. See *Liste des schaedlichen und unerwuenschten Schrifttums,* Stand vom 31. December 1938, Druck von Ernst Hedrich Nachf., in Leipzig. The novel came out for the first time in Germany in June 1969, (Frankfurt a.M.: S. Fischer Verlag), and was a great literary success. See "Die Stärke des Erstaunens" by Tadeusz Nowakowski in *Die Zeit,* Hamburg, June 20, 1969, and reviews in all the leading German and Austrian newspapers. (cf. my Bibliography.) In Austria and Germany Wittlin's book was selected "The Book of the Month."

4. "Die Stärke des Erstaunens," *Die Zeit,* June 20, 1969.

5. Julian Krzyzanowski, *Dzieje literatury polskiej.* (Warsaw: Panstwowe wydawnictwo naukowe, 1969).

6. *Ibid.,* p. 641.

7. "Wittlin, Józef," *Slownik wspólczesnych pisarzy polskich* (Warsaw: Panstwowe wydawnictwo naukowe, 1964), III, p. 513.

8. Czeslaw Milosz, *The History of Polish Literature* (London: The Macmillan Company, 1969), pp. 423-24.

9. See for instance Ryszard Matuszewski, *Contemporary Polish Writers* (Warsaw: Polonia Publishing House, 1959).

10. Joseph Wittlin, "Joseph Wittlin," *Books Abroad,* XVI, 1 (January, 1942), p. 4, henceforth referred to as "Joseph Wittlin."

11. "Forbidden Games" was the title of a French film of 1940 about children whose parents were killed during the war.

12. "Pisma posmiertne," *Orfeusz w piekle XX wieku (Orpheus in the Inferno of the Twentieth Century)* (Paris: Instytut Literacki, 1963), pp. 629-37. Henceforth referred to as *Orpheus.*

13. "Joseph Wittlin," p. 4.

14. *Orpheus*, p. 41.

15. *Orpheus*, p. 289.

16. *Orpheus*, p. 325.

17. "Joseph Wittlin," p. 5.

18. *Ibid.*

19. *Ibid.*, p. 5. Stanislaw Wyspianski (1869-1907) was a leading Polish Symbolist, poet, painter and dramatist.

20. Wilhelm Feldman, *Wspólczesna literatura polska* (Warsaw: Towarzystwo wydawnicze, 1919), III, p. 180 and *passim.*

21. Karol Klein, "Ekspresjonizm polski (Grupa Zdroju)," *Przeglad humanistyczny,* IV-V (1932), p. 458.

22. Jan Klossowicz, "Polscy ekspresjonisci," *Dialog,* V, 7 (1960), p. 113.

23. Klein lists the following names: Kandinsky, Marc, Helm, Werfel, Rubiner, Benn, Kokoschka, Lasker-Schueler, Lichtenstein, Kornfeld, Meyrink, Pinthus and Rilke (the last was considered a predecessor by the Expressionists).

24. Walter H. Sokel, *The Writer in Extremis. Expressionism in XX Century German Literature* (Los Angeles: Stanford University Press, 1959).

25. *Orpheus*, p. 435.

26. "Czego chcemy," *Zdroj (Source),* X, 5-6 (March, 1920), p. 60.

27. *Ibid.*, p. 59.

28. See Stanislaw Przybyszewski's article "Powrotna fala," *Zdrój,* VI (March, 1918), pp. 169-73.

29. Przybyszewski sums up the core of Slowacki's teachings in a long treatise "Ekspresjonism, Slowacki i Genezis z Ducha," *Zdrój,* V (December, 1918), p. 169, as follows: "Everything is created for the Spirit, by the Spirit and nothing exists for a bodily purpose." (Translation is mine, Z. Y.)

30. Przybyszewski, *op. cit. Zdrój,* V, 1 (1918), p. 6.

31. Klein, *op. cit.*, p. 472.

32. W. Kozicki, "Zmiennosc sadów i ocen estetycznych," *Skamander,* LVIII (May, 1935), p. 93.

33. Klein, *op. cit.*, p. 471 (my translation).

34. The Expressionists sought to express "the eternal history of the soul"; See the Expressionists' manifesto in *Zdrój* (May, 1920) as quoted by K. Klein, *op. cit.*, p. 471.

35. Klein, *op. cit.*, p. 473.

36. Jan Stur, "Z rozmyslan czlowieka na przelomie," *Zdrój*, V (June, 1920), p. 179.

37. Klein, *op. cit.*, p. 474.

38. *Orpheus*, p. 74 (my translation).

39. Jan Józef Lipski, "O ekspresjonizmie 'Hymnów'," reprinted in *Jan Kasprowicz*, ed. by Roman Loth (Warsaw: Panstwowe Zaklady Wydawnictw Szkolnych, 1964), pp. 287-94, *passim*.

40. Wittlin was called "muezzin" of his generation by Countess Nina Morstin, wife of a distinguished author who was Wittlin's close friend, Ludwik Hieronim Morstin, in whose house "Congresses of the Poets" were held in 1928 and 1929.

41. *Hymns* will be quoted in this book from texts supplied by Mr. Wittlin which differ somewhat from all three editions of the book, none of which, unfortunately, are available in U.S. libraries. (See Appendix for English translations of some of the *Hymns*.)

42. See English version of the hymn by Paul Mayewski in the *Introduction to Modern Polish Literature*, ed. by Adam Gillon and Ludwik Krzyzanowski (New York: Twayne Publishers, 1964), p. 412.

43. In an interview with me in December, 1966. A well known Polish émigré writer, Józef Mackiewicz, writes in his recent book *Lewa wolna* (London, 1965), (p. 236) that in war everything depends on one's intestines, on how they work. About the spirit of the soldiers one reads only in operation orders, remarks one of the characters in this book.

44. The reference is to an actual event, when Wittlin and his friend Jan Stur, the poet, were required to dig graves for those killed in Lwów during the fratricidal war. See *Orpheus*, p. 75.

45. This is reminiscent of one of Kasprowicz's *Hymns*.

46. *Sonnets to Orpheus*, quoted in *Orpheus*, p. 15.

47. Nicholas Gogol, "A Madman's Diary," in *Old Russian Stories*, selected by J. I. Rodale (Emmaus, Pa.: The Story Classics, 1951), p. 198.

48. Vsevolod Setchkarev, *Nicholas Gogol* (New York: New York University Press, 1965), p. 242.

49. *Introduction to Modern Polish Literature*, *op. cit.*, p. 415.

50. *Ibid.*, p. 417.

51. *Sovremennye pol'skie poety v ocherkakh Sergeia Kulakovskogo i v perevodakh Mikhaila Khoromanskogo* (Berlin: Petropolis, 1929), p. 128.

52. Northrop Frye, *Anatomy of Criticism* (New York: Atheneum, First Atheneum edition, 1966), p. 281.

53. Juliusz Kleiner, "Hymny Józefa Wittlina," *Gazeta wieczorna*, (Lwów), No. 5556 (1920).

54. *Ibid.*

55. W. Sokel, *op. cit.*, p. 172.

56. Pawel Hulka-Laskowski, "Poeta pokoju i milosci," *Wiadomosci literackie*, II (1928).

57. Kleiner, *op. cit.*

58. Klein, *op. cit.*, p. 464.

Chapter Two

1. Stanislaw Lam, ed. *Najwybitniejsi poeci emigracji wspólczesnej* (Paris: Ksiegarnia Polska w Paryzu, n.d.), pp. 167-93.

2. The Polish poet Jan Kochanowski (1530-1584), the greatest poet during the Slavic Renaissance era, composed a series of 19 Laments (Threnos) after the death of his daughter, Ursula. They were acclaimed as the crowning achievement of his creativity. Wittlin "added" a Lament XX, stylizing it superbly to harmonize with Kochanowski's first nineteen.

3. In the Warsaw ghetto dead bodies were actually covered with paper for lack of linen and shrouds.

4. We find the grotesque story of Anna Csillag also in a prose excerpt by Bruno Szulc (Schulz), "Ksiega," *Skamander*, LVIII (May, 1935) pp. 102-3 and *passim*. Szulc was fond of listening to Wittlin's recitations of his poems and prose.

5. Pong's expression: see R. Wellek and A. Warren, *Theory of Literature* (A Harvest book, New York: Harcourt, Brace and World, Inc.), pp. 193-94.

6. Similar images can be found in the poetry of several Russian and Polish poets and writers such as Lermontov, Chekhov, Bely, Julian Tuwim and others. Wittlin uses it also in *The Salt of the Earth*. See Chapter V.

7. See Reiss' translation in the Appendix to this book.

8. We remember "manna" from the "Prelude" to the *Hymns*, see Appendix.

9. Jan Bielatowicz, "Pisarz najcichszych tonów," *Wiadomosci*, XXXVII (1963).

10. *Orpheus*, pp. 417-21.

11. *Orpheus*, p. 474.

12. *Orpheus*, p. 75.

13. Franciszek Siedlecki, "Z dziejów naszego wiersza," *Skamander*, LXII (September, 1935), p. 432.

14. Jan Stur, "Z rozmyslan czlowieka na przelomie," *Zdrój*, V (June, 1920), p. 179.

Chapter Three

1. *Wiadomosci literackie*, XX (1931).

2. An English translation of the drama was recently published,

Stanislaw Wyspianski. *The Return of Odysseus.* Tr. with an Introduction by Howard Clarke (Indiana University Publications, Russian
and East European Series, 35 Bloomington, 1966). It was reviewed
in *The Slavic and East European Journal,* Summer 1968, vol. XII,
No. 2, p. 247.

3. " 'Odysseja' w oblezonym Lwowie," *Wiadomosci literackie,* XX
(1931).

4. "The Name of Odysseus," *Essays on the Odyssey,* ed. by Charles
Taylor, Jr. (Bloomington, Indiana: Indiana University Press, 1963),
p. 66.

5. I shall refer henceforth to the three versions of Wittlin's *Odyssey*
as *Odyssey I* (1924), *Odyssey II* (1931) and *Odyssey III* (1957).
For other publication facts see bibliography at the end of the book.

6. *Orpheus,* pp. 564-65.

7. He was criticized by Witold Doroszewski, "Uwagi o ostatnim
przekladzie 'Odyseji'," *Sprawozdania Towarzystwa Naukowego War-
szawskiego* (1933), pp. 71-83. Objections to Wittlin's language in the
translation of the *Odyssey* were also voiced by: Stanislaw Seliga in
Przeglad humanistyczny, zeszyt 4 (1924); Waclaw Borowy in "Dawni
teoretycy tlumaczen," *O sztuce tlumaczenia* (The Art of Translating)
ed. by M. Rusinek (Wroclaw: Zaklad im. Ossolinskich, 1955), pp.
36-37; Tadeusz Sinko (see especially his Preface to the 6th edition
of the *Odyssey* translated by L. Siemienski, Seria II Biblioteki Naro-
dowej, Wroclaw: Zaklad im. Ossolinskich, 1959). However, elsewhere
Sinko (cf. his *Literatura grecka,* Cz. I, Kraków, 1931) praised poetic
qualities and freshness of expression in Wittlin's translation, Krystyna
Stawecka compared Wittlin's *Odyssey III* with Jan Parandowski's
prose translation (see "Dwa polskie przeklady 'Odyseji'," *Roczniki
humanistyczne,* Lublin, t. IX, zeszyt 2, 1961) and came to the conclusion that in spite of the prose translation's greater accuracy, a
poetic rendering of Homer's epic is to be preferred.

8. E.g. Lucjan Siemienski in his Homer, *Odysseja* (Warsaw:
Gebethner i Wolf, 1903). The translation appeared first in 1873.

9. Polish hexameters in translating Homer were used, among others,
by: Augustyn Szmurlo for the *Iliad,* (Warsaw, 1887); Stanislaw
Mleczko, for the *Iliad* (Warsaw, 1894), for the *Odyssey* only in 1935,
i.e., *after* Wittlin's *Odyssey II* was published. Another rendering of the
Odyssey in hexameters by Antoni Bronikowski appeared in 2 volumes
(in 1859 and in 1867 respectively, in Poznan) and was a total failure.
For description of the Polish hexameter see Maria Dluska, *Studia z
historii i teorii wersyfikacji polskiej* (Kraków: Polska Akademia Umie-
jetnosci. Prace Komisji Jezykowej No. 35), pp. 148-55.

10. Józef Wittlin, Preface to *Odyssey I,* pp. 38-39.

11. *Ibid.*

12. George de F. Lord, *Homeric Renaissance. The Odyssey of George Chapman* (New Haven: Yale University Press, 1956), p. 30.

13. Preface to *Odyssey III*, p. 25: "super-prosaic" meant a translation unlawfully used by high school students in Galician school argot.

14. *Ibid.*

15. *Ibid.*

16. *Ibid.*, p. 26.

17. *Ibid.*, p. 27.

18. Nikolai Gogol, *Selected Passages from Correspondence with Friends*, tr. by Jesse Zeldin (Nashville, Tennessee: Vanderbilt University Press, 1969), p. 39 and p. 41.

19. See *Orpheus*, essays devoted to the *Odyssey* and polemics with Jan Parandowski and others: pp. 562-80 and pp. 580-84.

20. Thus "ocemgnieniu" or "oczymgnieniu" is faulty because a singular should be used: "*okam*gnieniu" (in the twinkling of *an* eye).

21. E. V. Rieu, tr. Homer, *The Odyssey* (Baltimore: Penguin Books, 1965), p. 11.

22. *Ibid.*, p. 171.

23. Victor Erlich, *Russian Formalism. History-Doctrine* (Hague: Mouton and Co., 1955), p. 55.

24. Wittlin has said this repeatedly in interviews with me, for instance in December, 1965.

25. Pawel Hostowiec, "Nowe wydanie 'Soli ziemi'," *Kultura*, VII-VIII (1955), where several parallels between Wittlin's *Odyssey* and *The Salt of the Earth* are drawn. See also Chapter V of this book.

26. Józef Wittlin, Preface to *Odyssey III*, p. 37.

27. S. Srebrny, "Nowa polska 'Odyseja'," *Wiadomosci literackie*, L (1932).

28. [Zygmunt Kubiak], "Polski Homer," *Tygodnik powszechny*, September 22, 1957.

29. *Orpheus*, pp. 569-70.

30. *O sztuce tlumaczenia* ed. by M. Rusinek, p. 553.

31. Zofia Kozarynowa, "Przeklady z jezyków obcych," *Literatura polska na obczyznie 1940-1960*, ed. by Tymon Terlecki (London: B. Swiderski, 1965), II, pp. 359-60.

32. Pawel Hostowiec, "Odyseja w nowym tlumaczeniu Wittlina," *Kultura*, XI (1957), p. 141.

Chapter Four

1. As quoted by Ludwik Fryde, *Wybór pism krytycznych*, ed. by Andrzej Bielecki (Warsaw: Panstwowy Instytut Wydawniczy, 1966), p. 393.

2. E. W. Van O'Connor, ed., *Forms of Modern Fiction* (Bloomington, Indiana: Indiana University Press, 1964), p. 25.

3. V. Zhirmunskii, *Voprosy teorii literatury* (Problems of the Theory of Literature) (S. 'Gravenhage: Mouton & Co., 1962), p. 17.

4. K. Zawodzinski, "Die zeitgenossische Literatur Polens," *Slavische Rundschau*, V (1933), p. 230-42, as quoted by Zbigniew Folejewski in *Maria Dabrowska* (New York: Twayne Publishers, Inc., 1967), p. 99.

5. At that time Wittlin, who incidentally possesses absolute pitch, had already successfully staged chorus performances of Euripides in the Municipal Theatre of Lodz, directing the choruses himself.

6. Fryde, *op. cit.*, p. 403.

7. Kazimierz Wyka, in a book review of *The Salt of the Earth* in *Droga*, XI (1935), p. 998.

8. Jan Lorentowicz, "Liryk i jego epos," *Echo spoleczne*, No. 4/5 (1936).

9. P. Zdziechowski, "Ksiazka o wojnie," *Bunt mlodych*, III (1936).

10. Emil Breiter, "Odwet serca," *Wiadomosci literackie*, XLIII (1935).

11. Leon Piwinski, "Powiesc," *Rocznik literacki 1935*, (Warsaw, 1936), pp. 87-89.

12. Ankieta Wiadomosci literackich, *Wiadomosci literackie*, LII (1933).

13. "Józef Wittlin," an interview with M. Down, *Wiadomosci literackie*, LXI (1936).

14. Northrop Frye, *Anatomy of Criticism* (New York: Atheneum, 1966), p. 13.

15. Zofia Starowiejska-Morstinowa, *Ci, których spotykalam* (Cracow: Znak, 1962).

16. Alfred Kazin, "Books and Things," *New York Herald Tribune*, October 25, 1941.

17. T. Terlecki, ed., *Literatura polska na obczyznie 1940-1960* (London: B. Swiderski, 1965), I, p. 158.

18. Józef Wittlin, "O 'epopei' Delteil'a *Les poilus*," *Wiadomosci literackie*, IV (1927).

19. *Ibid.*

20. A parallel with the great nineteenth century Russian writer Nikolai Gogol comes to mind. Gogol, who was preparing a handbook on the theory of literature, describes in it a "minor epic," in which the hero is neither a demiurge nor a hero in the accepted sense, but an ordinary man whose life, however, might be of interest in its way. Gogol subtitled his own "minor epic" of Russia *Dead Souls*, a "poem."

21. *Wiadomosci literackie,* XII (1924) and *Wiadomosci literackie,* CCXXIV (1928), and other essays.

22. J. Wittlin, "Epopea w kinie," *Wiadomosci literackie,* CCXXIV (1928).

23. An interview with J. Wittlin, *Wiadomosci literackie,* XII (1924).

24. Percy Lubbock, *The Craft of Fiction* (New York: The Viking Press, 1957), p. 35.

25. I was very glad to find my views confirmed in the *Nachwort* by the talented German writer Peter Härtling to the new German edition of *The Salt of the Earth,* (Frankfurt: Fischer Verlag, 1969.)

26. A. Döblin, "Ein polnischer 'Soldat Schweyk'—Zu Joseph Wittlin's Roman *Das Salz der Erde,*" Pariser Tageszeitung, No. 139, October 28, 1936. It is interesting to note that a Czech translator of *The Salt of the Earth* prefers it to Hasek's celebrated novel.

27. See Chapter V of this book.

28. Fryde, *op. cit.,* pp. 408-10.

29. Wittlin was the first, to my knowledge, to create a demiurge out of the Austrian Emperor Franz Josef. Joseph Roth's portrayal of the Emperor in *Radetzky Marsch* resembles somewhat Wittlin's description.

30. These quotations are taken from the new translation of a part of Wittlin's Prologue to *The Salt of the Earth* as it appeared in the *Introduction to Modern Polish Literature,* ed. by Adam Gillon and Ludwik Krzyzanowski (New York: Twayne Publishers, 1964). All other quotations are taken from the translation by Pauline de Chary (New York: Sheridan House Publishers, 1941) with the page enclosed in parentheses following the quotation for the convenience of the reader.

31. Wiktor Weintraub, "Literatura nezavisimoi Pol'shi," (The Literature of Independent Poland), *The New Review* (Novyi Zhurnal), XXXII (1953), p. 168.

32. See Wittlin's poem "Zolnierz znany," *Skamander,* XLIII (January, 1926), p. 23-25, in which he mocks "the necrophiles of history." See also *Orpheus,* p. 29.

33. See Fryde's article *op. cit.* on Expressionistic features of *The Salt of the Earth,* pp. 399-402 and *passim.*

34. P. Lubbock, *op. cit.,* p. 115 and *passim.*

35. A. Doeblin, *op. cit.*

36. *Ibid.*

37. The passage has been retranslated with a view to keeping the text closer to the original.

38. On satiric distortion see Gilbert Highet, *The Anatomy of Satire* (Princeton, N. J.: Princeton University Press, 1962), pp. 156-58.

39. The epithet "shaggy" (kudlaty) appears in Wittlin's Polish *Odyssey.*

40. St. Luke: XVI. 19-31.

41. Such a human sacrifice is made in the second part of Wittlin's trilogy, entitled *The Healthy Death.*

42. There is some resemblance between this scene and the one in the *Book of the Dead* in the *Odyssey.*

Chapter Five

1. As quoted by W. K. Wimsatt, Jr. *The Verbal Icon. Studies in the Meaning of Poetry* (The Noonday Press: Third Noonday Paperbound Edition, 1962), p. 111.

2. Wit Tarnawski, "Po dwudziestu latach," *Mysl Polska,* No. 14 (1956).

3. The Polish original has an "angel" instead of "her." To Wittlin the sound of the corresponding Polish word "aniol" seems to suggest its *Gestalt:* cf. Preface to *Odyssey II.*

4. Fryde, *op. cit.,* p. 400.

5. C. G. Jung, *Modern Man in Search of a Soul* (New York: Harcourt, Brace & World, Inc., A Harvest Book), p. 168.

6. David Lodge, *The Language of Fiction* (New York: Columbia University Press, 1966), p. 47.

7. Northrop Frye, *op. cit.,* p. 228.

8. I have been told by Mr. Wittlin of the gist of the contents of the two later volumes of his Trilogy.

9. I. Strohschneider-Kohrs, *Die Romantische Ironie in Theorie und Gestaltung* (Tuebingen: Max Niemeyer, 1960), p. 212.

10. N. Frye, *op. cit.,* p. 223.

11. See *The Salt of the Earth,* pp. 66-67 and *passim.*

12. A statement made in an interview with me in October, 1956.

13. See also my article on Wittlin in Russian in *The New Review (Novyi Zhurnal)* published in New York, vol. XLVII (Dec., 1956), p. 100.

14. C. G. Jung, *op. cit.,* p. 145.

15. Thomas Mann wrote in a letter of October 5, 1941 to Wittlin's American publisher about *The Salt of the Earth:* "It belongs, in my opinion, to the small number of contemporary narrative works which, despite their modern criticism, extend into the sphere of the typical and thus the mythical and epical."

Chapter Six

1. Cf. Charles Neider, (ed.) *The Stature of Thomas Mann. An Anthology of Criticism* (New York: New Directions, 1947).

2. *For Your Freedom and Ours; Polish Progressive Spirit through*

the Centuries. Preface by Malcolm W. Davis, Translation and editorial
assistance by Ludwik Krzyzanowski (New York: Frederick Ungar
Publishing Company, 1943.) Another edition of this book by the same
editors has a slightly different title and a preface by Bertrand Russell:
The Democratic Heritage of Poland; "For Your Freedom and Ours."
(London: G. Allen & Unwin Ltd., 1944.) The book has appeared also
in Polish under the title: *Polska mysl demokratyczna w ciagu wieków,*
antologia w opracowaniu M. Kridla, W. Malinowskiego i J. Wittlina.
(Nowy York: "Polish Labor Group," London, Sklad główny "Nowa
Polska" "New Poland," 1945.)

    3. *For Your Freedom and Ours, op. cit.,* p. 358.

    4. Józef Wittlin, "Dar intelektu," *Kutura,* I-II (1965), p. 216-22.

    5. See Note 2 above.

    6. In the above mentioned article in *Kultura* (Note 4) "physiology"
has been erroneously replaced by "philosophy," (cf. p. 220 of the
Kultura article).

    7. Cf. "Literature in Exile" in *Essays in Comparative Literature* by
Herbert Dieckmann, Harry Levin, Helmut Motekat, (St. Louis, Mis-
souri: Washington University Studies, 1961).

    8. Wiktor Weintraub, "Mój Lwów," *Wiadomosci,* XXI/LX (1947).

    9. This "Reminiscence" was read in English in New York on the
Fifth Anniversary of his death. A German translation of the essay
appeared in *Joseph Roth. Leben und Werk.* Ein Gedächtnisbuch.
(Köln und Hagen: Verlag Gustav Kiepenheuer, 1949).

    10. Eduard Spranger, *Lebensformen* (Tübingen: Neomarius Ver-
lag, 1950), pp. 236 and ff.

    11. "Pan Tadeusz" in *Adam Mickiewicz, Poet of Poland,* ed. by
Manfred Kridl (New York: Columbia University Press, 1951).

Chapter Seven

    1. This has been stated by Juliusz Kleiner in his *Die polnische
Literatur,* 1929, as quoted by Karol Klein, "Ekspresjonizm polski
(Grupa Zdroju)," *Przeglad Humanistyczny,* IV-V (1932), pp. 464-65.

    2. Pawel Hostowiec, "Nowe wydanie 'Soli ziemi'," *Kultura,* VII-
VIII (1955), p. 201.

    3. Hermann Kesten, "Eine einfache Geschichte," *Der Monat,* V
(1969).

    4. See especially the beginning of Julian Stryjkowski's *Austeria*
(Warsaw: Czytelnik, 1966).

    5. Wittlin had defended Witold Gombrowicz against hostile criti-
cism as early as 1951. (cf. "Apologia Gombrowicza" in *Orpheus).*
Recently, before his untimely death, Gombrowicz won international

acclaim, was awarded France's famous Formentor prize, and won other distinctions. His books have been translated into all major European languages.

6. As quoted by Erich Heller in his *Thomas Mann. The Ironic German* (A Meridian book, Cleveland and New York: The World Publishing Company, 1961), p. 209.

Selected Bibliography

PRIMARY SOURCES

I. BOOKS

Hymny. Poznan: Nakladem Zdroju, 1920.

Hymny. Warsaw: Pod znakiem poetów. Seria nowa. J. Mortkowicz, 1929.

Powiesc o cierpliwym piechurze. Cz. I. Sól ziemi. 5th ed. New York: Roy Publishers, 1954.

Orfeusz w piekle XX wieku. Pisma I. Paris: Instytut Literacki, 1963.

Poems in *Najwybitniejsi poeci emigracji,* ed. by Stanislaw Lam. Paris: Ksiegarnia Polska w Paryzu, /n.d./

II. ARTICLES IN POLISH

"Festiwal muzyczno-teatralny w Wiedniu," *Wiadomosci literackie,* XLIV (1924).

"Sztuka polska na wystawie w Wenecji," *Wiadomosci literackie,* CXXVII (1926).

"Swiety Fransiszek z Assyzu. Aksamit Truwera. *Skamander,* XLIX (1927).

"O swietym Franciszku z Assyzu," *Wiadomosci literackie,* XLIII (1927).

"Przedmowa do nowego wydania 'Hymnów'," *Wiadomosci literackie,* CLXXVIII (1927).

"O 'epopei' Delteila 'Les poilus'," *Wiadomosci literackie,* CLV (1927).

"Amerykanski Shaw (W. W. Woodward)," *Wiadomosci literackie,* CCXIV (1928).

"O przyszlosc Europy" (Bruno Franka 'Politische Novelle'), *Wiadomosci literackie,* CCXXII (1928).

"Walka z klamstwem" (Kurt Tucholsky 'Mit 5 PS.'), *Wiadomosci literackie,* CCXXIV (1928).

"Powiesc Arnolda Zweiga o jencu Griszy," *Wiadomosci literackie,* CCLV (1928).

"Fortunat Strowski o Ameryce ('La Bruyère en Amerique')," *Wiadomosci literackie*, CCIC (1929).
"Europa przeciw ojczyznom (Drieu la Rochelle: 'L'Europe contre les patries'," *Wiadomosci literackie*, CDIII (1931).
"O nawróceniu sw. Franciszka," *Kultura* (Warsaw), VII (1932).
"Sw. Franciszek na wojnie," *Tygodnik ilustrowany*, XXV-XXVIII (1932).
"Jezyk Prusa," *Wiadomosci literackie*, CDXVIII (1932).
"Chiny prosza o glos," *Wiadomosci literackie*, CDXXXV (1932).
" 'Rzeczpospolita poetów' Morstina," *Wiadomosci literackie*, XXIV (1934).
"Nowy Sybir," *Wiadomosci literackie*, XXVI (1934).
"W stulecie 'Pana Tadeusza'," *Wiadomosci literackie*, DLV (1934).
" 'Klub kawalerów' i 'Zielone pudla'," *Wiadomosci literackie*, XXX (1934).
"Genius loci i Czermanski," *Wiadomosci literackie*, XVIII (1935).
"Maly komentarz do 'Soli ziemi'," *Wiadomosci literackie*, VI (1936).
"Bylem tam, gdzie sie zaczela inwazja," *Tygodnik polski* (New York), XXVI (1944).
Preface to: W. Gombrowicz: *Trans-Atlantyk. Slub*. Paris: Instytut Literacki, 1953.
"Mloda proza emigracyjna," *Wiadomosci*, XXXIV (1959).
Preface to: Pawel Mayewski. *Rzeka*. tr. by Jan Kempke. London: Oficyna poetów i malarzy, 1960.
"Pegazy na Kredytowej." *Wiadomosci*, XXIII (1964).
"Dar intelektu," *Kultura* (Paris), I-II (1965).
"Z Rafalem i o Rafale." *Wiadomosci*. XV (1966).
"Na pozegnanie Wierzynskiego," *Kultura* (Paris), IV (1969).
"Epitafium," *Wiadomosci*, XXVI-XXVII (1969).

III. ARTICLES IN ENGLISH

"Poles of Stature," *Saturday Review of Literature*, XXV, 4 (1942).
"The Perception of Hell," *Saturday Review of Literature*, XXX, 24 (1947) also in Neider, Charles (ed.), *The Stature of Thomas Mann. An Anthology of Criticism*. New York: New Directions, 1947, as "On Poetic Fiction."
"Tadeusz Kosciuszko," in Ludwig, Emil and Kranz, Henry B., *The Torch of Freedom. Twenty Exiles of History*. New York: Farrar-Rinehart, 1943.
"Pan Tadeusz," in *Adam Mickiewicz. Poet of Poland. A Symposium*. Ed. by Manfred Kridl, New York: Columbia University Press, 1951.
"Sorrow and Grandeur of Exile," *Polish Review*, II, 2-3 (1957), also as "The Splendor and the Squalor of Exile," in *Explorations in Freedom; Prose, Narrative, and Poetry from Kultura*, ed. Leopold

Tyrmand. New York: Free Press, a Division of the Macmillan Company, 1970.

"Poe in the Bronx," tr. R. Langer, *Polish Review*, IV, 1-2 (1959).

"Gogol's Inferno," *Polish Review*, VII, 4 (1962).

"A Quarter Century of Polish Literature," (1927-1952), *Books Abroad*, XXX (1956).

"Epilogue" in *For Your Freedom and Ours. Polish Progressive Spirit through the Centuries.* ed. M. Kridl, W. Malinowski and J. Wittlin. Translation and editorial assistance by Ludwik Krzyzanowski. New York: Frederick Ungar Publishing Company, 1943.

IV. ARTICLE IN ITALIAN

"L'inferno di Gogol," Tempo Presente, Anno V, No. 1 (1960).

V. WORKS TRANSLATED INTO FOREIGN LANGUAGES

Sól ziemi

Czech: tr. and preface by Jaroslav Zavada, Praha: "Sfinx," Bohumil Janda, 1937.

Croatian: tr. J. Benesic, Zagreb: Sovremenna Biblioteka 9, 1940.

Dutch: tr. A. E. Boutelje. Amsterdam, 1937.

English: tr. Pauline de Chary. London: Methuen, 1939. 2nd edition London, 1940; New York: Sheridan House, 1941. 3rd edition Harrisburg, Pa.: Giniger-Stackpole Books, 1970.

French: tr. Henry Raymond. Paris: Albin Michel, 1939.

German: tr. Dr. I. Berman. Amsterdam: Allert de Lange, 1937. 2nd edition Frankfurt am Main: S. Fischer Verlag, 1969. 3rd edition Frankfurt am Main, Wien, Zurich: Büchergilde Gutenberg, 1970.

Hebrew: tr. B. Tannenbaum. Tel-Aviv: Gazith, 1943.

Hungarian: Bratislava: Prager, 1939.

Italian: tr. Janina Gromska. Milano: Bompiani, 1st edition 1939; 4th ed. 1945.

Russian: tr. E. Gonzago. Moscow: Vsemirnaia biblioteka 67/69, 1937.

Russian: tr. E. Tropowski, Leningrad, 1937.

Swedish: tr. Göran Salander. Stockholm: Wahlström and Widstrand, 1939.

Spanish: tr. Leon Mirlas. Buenos Aires: Editora Inter Americana, 1945.

Hymny

Hebrew: tr. B. Tannenbaum. Tel-Aviv: Gazith, 1943.

VI. POEMS IN FOREIGN LANGUAGE ANTHOLOGIES

Poetry of Freedom. William Rose Benet and Norman Cousins (eds.), Toronto: Random House, 1945 and 1948.

Polnische Poesie des 20. Jahrhunderts. Ed. by Karl Dedecius, Darmstadt: Moderner Buch-Club, 1965.
Poeti polacchi contemporanei. Tr. by Carlo Verdiani. Genoa, 1961.
Anthologie de la Poésie Polonaise. Editions du Seuil, Paris, 1965.
Sovremennye pol'skie poety v ocherkakh Sergeia Kulakovskogo i v perevodakh Mikhaila Khoromanskogo. Berlin: Petropolis, 1929.

VII. TRANSLATIONS INTO POLISH BY WITTLIN

Homer. *Odyseja.* Lwów: H. Altenberg. Zaklad Narodowy im Ossolinskich, 1924.
Homer. *Odyseja. Warszawa-Kraków.* Wydawnictwo J. Mortkowisza. T-wo Wydawnicze w Warszawie, 1931.
Homer. *Odyseja.* London: Veritas, 1957.
John Hersey. *Hiroszima.* Warsaw: Spóldzielnia Wydawnicza "Wiedza," 1948.

For other articles and translations and adaptations see *Slownik współczesnych pisarzy polskich.* Warsaw: Panstowe Wydawnictwo Naukowe, 1964, III, 512-17.

ARTICLES ABOUT WITTLIN

Andrzejewski, Jerzy. "Szary czlowiek i 'Sól ziemi'," *Prosto z mostu,* III (1936). A perceptive book review of *The Salt of the Earth.*
Bielatowicz, Jan. "Pisarz najcichszych tonów," *Wiadomosci,* XXXVII (1963). An excellent, beautifully written essay on Wittlin's *Orpheus in the Inferno of the Twentieth Century.*
Breza, Tadeusz. "Piekna ksiazka J. Wittlina," *Kurier Poranny,* No. 344 (1935). A concise book review of *The Salt of the Earth,* containing valuable remarks on its epic qualities and humor.
Coleman, Arthur. "Joseph Wittlin," *Saturday Review,* August 2, 1941. Lavish in its praise of Wittlin.
Cournos, John. "A Prize-Winning Novel from Poland," *The New York Times Book Review,* October 5, 1941. A well-known critic and translator discovers Wittlin and his novel.
Döblin, Alfred. "Ein polnischer Soldat Schwejk," *Pariser Tageszeitung,* October 28, 1936. A sympathetic assessment of *The Salt of the Earth* by a well-known German writer, then an émigré. Comparisons with Jaroslav Hasek's novel are drawn.
Folejewski, Zbigniew. "The Creative Path of Joseph Wittlin," *The Polish Review,* IX, No. 1 (1964), pp. 67-72. A general appraisal of Wittlin's work.
Fryde, Ludwik. "O prozie Wittlina," *Ateneum,* III (1939). The best critical study on Wittlin's *Salt of the Earth* containing perceptive remarks on his poetry and on his entire creative output.

Härtling, Peter. "Joseph Wittlin: Das Salz der Erde." *Die Welt der Literatur*, (Hamburg), January 20, 1962. A German novelist and critic of distinction discovers Wittlin's novel in the German Amsterdam edition, is captivated and praises it highly.

Hostowiec, Pawel./J. Stempowski/. "Nowe wydanie 'Soli ziemi'," *Kultura*, VII-VIII (1955). A perceptive review of the new Polish edition of *The Salt of the Earth*, including interesting remarks on reminiscences of classical antiquity in the novel.

Hulka-Laskowski, Pawel. "Poeta pokoju i milosci," *Wiadomosci literackie*, II (1928). A stimulating review of Wittlin's *Hymns*.

Hyman, Stanley. "The Patient Foot-Soldier," *The New Republic*, October 27, 1941. A well-known American critic writes an enlightening essay on *The Salt of the Earth* calling it "a novel to rank easily with the best war literature of our time."

Kazin, Alfred. "Books and Things," ed. by Lewis Gannett, *The New York Herald Tribune*, October 25, 1941. Kazin praises Wittlin's "grand style" and compares *The Salt of the Earth* to Dos Passos' *1919*.

Kesten, Hermann. "Eine einfache Geschichte," *Der Monat*, V (1969). An account of Wittlin and his novel in interview form by a German writer.

Kleiner, Juliusz. "Hymny Wittlina," *Gazeta wieczorna*, (Lwów), No. 5554 and No. 5556 (1920). An excellent analysis of Wittlin's *Hymns* by a Polish literary scholar of international renown.

Kridl, Manfred. "World War I," *Decision* (Jan.-Feb., 1942). A Polish scholar of distinction puts *The Salt of the Earth* into a broad context of war literature.

Kubiak, Zygmunt. "Polski Homer," *Tygodnik Powszechny*, September 22, 1957. A well-known critic and classical philologist praises Wittlin's newest translation of *The Odyssey*.

Nowakowski, Tadeusz. "Die Stärke des Erstaunens," *Die Zeit*, (Hamburg), June 20, 1969. An enlightening essay on Wittlin's novel by a Polish émigré writer of the younger generation.

Sakowski, J. "Witamina duszy," *Wiadomosci*, XII (1956). A stimulating analysis of *Orpheus in the Inferno of the Twentieth Century*.

Srebrny, S. "Nowa polska 'Odyseja'," *Wiadomosci literackie*, L (1932). An expert review of Wittlin's *Odyssey*, 2nd version of 1931.

Stur, Jan. "Z rozmyslan czlowieka na przelomie," *Zdrój*, V (June, 1920). A penetrating assessment of Wittlin's *Hymns* by a leading Polish Expressionist.

Szenessy, Mario. "Stürmischer Bedacht," *Stuttgarter Zeitung*, June 28, 1969. A young German novelist praises *The Salt of the Earth*.

Weiskopf, F. C. "Joseph Wittlin. Salt of the Earth." *Books Abroad*, (Spring 1942). An insightful book review of Wittlin's novel.

Weintraub, Wiktor. "Mój Lwów," *Wiadomosci*. XXI/LX (1947). A perceptive appraisal of Wittlin's *Mój Lwów* by a leading Slavic scholar from Harvard University.

Wieniewski, Ignacy. "Wittlina przeklad 'Odyssei'," *Wiadomosci*, XLVII (1957). A classical philologist and translator of the *Iliad* expertly criticizes Wittlin's newest *Odyssey*, calling it a "magnum opus" of Polish émigré literature.

Zawodzinski, Karol W. *Opowiesci o powiesci*. Ed. by C. Zgorzelski. Cracow: Wydawnictwo literackie, 1963. A few pages of penetrating analysis of *The Salt of the Earth*.

For a detailed bibliography of Wittlin and on Wittlin see *Slownik wspólczesnych pisarzy polskich*. Warsaw: Panstowe Wydawnictwo Naukowe, 1964, III, pp. 512-17.

Index

85789

DATE